d below.

DARWIN AND THE SPIRIT OF MAN

With homage to the genius of
ALFRED RUSSEL WALLACE, OM, FRS
(1823–1913)
whom we should never forget
and who called his most important book on evolution
by just one word, *Darwinism*, and in it
(as we shall record on our p. 69) claimed to be
more Darwinian than Darwin

CONTENTS

ACKNOWLEDGEMENTS

All quotations are acknowledged, with reference to their publication and date, where they occur in the course of the book.

Regarding the work of the Religious Experience Research Unit which I set up at Manchester College, Oxford in 1969, the results of which are described in Chapter 12, I wish to make a special acknowledgement to those who worked with me. Originally I had intended this statement to be part of Chapter 12 itself, but I have been strongly advised to place it here so as not to interrupt the continuing flow of the argument. I want to make it clear that our results were obtained by the joint efforts of those working with me for different periods of time; their various lines of research have been discussed in my former book *The Spiritual Nature of Man*, so that here I will just give their names in gratitude for their devotion to the project.

Edward Robinson was my Deputy since almost the beginning and followed me as Director when I retired in 1976, Timothy Beardsworth was with me for several years, whilst Michael Walker and Brian Carter could only be with me for one year each; then Mrs Vita Toon gave invaluable help as curator of our records. Later we were able to appoint Miss Ann Morisy as sociological assistant to Mr David Hay, who, as recorded in Chapter 12, worked on the random sampling of experiences. The Oxford University Press are now issuing a new paperback edition of *The Spiritual Nature of Man* in which, in addition to accounts of their different fields of work, will be found references to their various publications.

In this volume I would also like to express my deep gratitude to my sister-in-law, Miss Ruth Garstang, formerly Bursar of Somerville College, who, for so many years since her retirement, has typed the manuscripts of my books. I want to record, as she feels at last that she must give it up, how much I am indebted to her for the skill, patience and good humour with which she has wrestled with my handwriting.

I must now thank Miss Vera Brice, a book designer of Collins Publishers, for all the trouble she has taken in preparing and arranging my typescript for its most advantageous and attractive appearance on the printed page. And finally I must say how grateful I am for the careful independent proof correcting, done in parallel to my own, by Miss Anita Jo Dunn, who has also collaborated with me in compiling the index.

1

Introduction

The theme of this book is certainly topical. It is so on two counts, quite apart from the fact that the year in which I began writing it was the centenary of Charles Darwin's death on 19 April 1882. I feel I must write it because the issues involved are so vital for our society, yet are not, or so it seems to me, being discussed in all their implications.

Firstly, few ideas have had a greater influence on the intellectual world of today than the supposition that the doctrine of Darwinian evolution must lead inevitably to a materialistic interpretation of life. This belief has been heightened by the discovery that the genetic code which governs the physical characteristics of all living organisms, including man, is based upon the same kind of complex, chemical molecule, the DNA (for short); and further, that the arrangement of parts of this remarkable molecule will from time to time undergo what appear to be random changes which alter the code governing individual variation. This is the neo-Darwinian position.

At first sight it does indeed look like a soulless automatic process which suggests to many people that all the qualities of life will ultimately be reduced to physical and chemical terms. In the last few years, however, we have seen among some of those engaged in higher education a growing concern with the increase in this *reductionism*, as it is called, and its influence upon our society. I am myself a neo-Darwinian, but I am convinced that this system does not explain all our qualities or indeed the whole of the process of evolution. Hence my urge to write, and not only on this score, but on the second also, for, as I have indicated, there are two main reasons for this subject being topical. We are now witnessing a new surge of interest, both in this country and America, as to the actual nature of the evolutionary process, or, in extreme examples, whether it has taken place at all.

The long series of letters on the subject in *The Times* and other journals, as well as programmes on television such as *Genesis hits back*, indicate a surprising diversity of views and a not infrequent lack of understanding of the real nature of the Darwinian doctrine. The use of the name Darwin in the title of my book is intended to represent not only the views of Darwin himself, but the development of his and Wallace's joint theory of natural selection and its subsequent combination with Mendel's laws of heredity which in turn have led to the modern concept of the genetic code. Darwin here stands for the present-day neo-Darwinian position. There are two important ways in which many of those letters and articles have shown a misconception of the Darwinian theory which I should like to point out at the very beginning.

For one thing, again and again in the argument the term Darwinism has been confused with the problem of the origin of life. Darwinian evolution is not concerned with a speculation as to how life actually began, although some may try to extend it into the realm of the chemical diversity which eventually gave rise to the possibility of a vehicle capable of carrying forward the living process. Darwinism deals with the gradual evolution of new forms of life from the very simplest organisms imaginable, not with the problem of how these very simple creatures became actually alive. It may be well to remind ourselves of the last sentence in Darwin's great book *The Origin of Species*; one which he left unchanged in the sixth and last edition. In ending his conclusions with a summary of his theory, he writes:

There is a grandeur in this view of life, with its several powers, having been originally breathed by the Creator into a few forms or into one; and that, whilst this planet

12

has gone cycling on according to the fixed law of gravity, from so simple a beginning endless forms most beautiful and most wonderful have been and are being evolved.

I quote this sentence only to show that he was clearly concerned with the gradual evolution of existing forms of life and not with the origin of life itself. Whilst he speaks of life being breathed into such forms by the Creator, I should point out that his views on the nature of God underwent a change in later life as shown in the first complete version of his *Autobiography* (with original omissions restored), edited and published by his grand-daughter, Nora Barlow (Collins, 1958). I will refer again to his theological views much later in the book (p. 168).

Another misunderstanding of Darwinian evolution has been evident in the recent discussion in the media; it concerns the rate of evolutionary change which some geologists have been saying has, in certain periods, been too rapid to be explained by the process of natural selection acting upon the small variations postulated in the neo-Darwinian theory. Instead, they go back to the idea of sudden jumps being the cause of evolutionary changes; an introductory chapter, however, is not the place for a discussion of this point, but I will come back to it in subsequent chapters (pp. 37 and 84).

Not only has there been a long series of letters in the general periodicals but also in scientific journals such as *Nature*. So extraordinary was this correspondence from scientists themselves that Sir Andrew Huxley (grandson of T.H.) devoted his presidential address to the Royal Society to the subject in 1981. Much of this correspondence was dealing with what is now technically known as 'cladistics' and Sir Andrew began his address by saying, 'Until a year or so ago few of us would have heard of "cladistics" and fewer still would have known what it is.' He went on to explain that it is a method of classifying organisms; this again, however, is not the place to go into such details, which many people do not feel to be fundamental to the evolutionary process. Referring further to this correspondence, Sir Andrew said he found himself being asked by scientists whether zoologists had ceased to believe in evolution, so that he began to wonder whether he ought to take up the cudgels on Darwin's behalf as T. H. Huxley did in his reply to Bishop Wilberforce at the 1860 meeting of the British Association. Now let me quote a short passage from his address:

At this year's meeting of the British Association in September, Sir Edmund Leach (1981), in a review of the progress of anthropology during the hundred and fifty years' existence of the Association, called attention to supposed anti-Darwinian tendencies among present-day biologists and claimed that 'many well-qualified scientists of the highest standing would today accept many of Wilberforce's criticisms of Darwin' . . . So the public is still being given the impression on all sides that scientists no longer believe in evolution. This is so far from the truth, and many of the arguments that have been used are so fallacious, that I have felt that I ought to take the opportunity of this address to put the record straight, in spite of the risks in speaking on a topic outside my own speciality, and of the risk that I may seem to be flogging a dead horse. Midway in the *Nature* correspondence, a letter from the Oxford zoologist J. R. Baker (1981) said 'We have slipped back a hundred years: how long before letters signed Wilberforce and Huxley appear?'. Leach has now come out as the champion of Wilberforce, and here is a Huxley answering the challenge.[1]

[1] On 9 September 1982 *The Times* published a front page article by its science correspondent reporting a debate at the British Association under the title 'New heretics cast doubt on Darwinism'; Sir Andrew, as President of the Royal Society, at once wrote a letter (published 11 September) saying that 'the article is highly misleading. The supporters of "punctuated equilibria" and of "cladistics" do not in any way "cast doubt on Darwinism"'. I need not discuss the meaning of the former term; Sir Andrew does so in his letter.

Since most of my earlier practical research has been concerned with marine ecology, which can hardly be regarded as grounds for writing on either evolution or man's spiritual nature, I feel that perhaps I owe the reader some account of my qualifications in this respect and ask his or her indulgence in allowing me a little autobiography.

It may surprise my colleagues when I say that secretly I regard my marine work as very much a hobby compared with my deeper biological thoughts. The truth is that I love the sea, and am fascinated with the nature, life, behaviour and ecology of the tiny creatures of the plankton. Since I first became a professor at the University (or University College as it then was) of Hull in 1928, until I retired from the Linacre Chair of Zoology at Oxford in 1961, I have always given the advanced courses of lectures on evolution; and after that I have continued to lecture on the subject and so have kept myself actively in touch with recent developments.

In 1938 I first published on the subject with an essay 'Change and Choice', on the importance of choice of environment, in the book *Evolution: Essays on Aspects of Evolutionary Biology* edited by G. C. (later Sir Gavin) de Beer (Clarendon Press, Oxford). In 1942 my inaugural address, on being appointed to the Regius Chair of Natural History in the University of Aberdeen, was entitled and published as *Natural History Old and New*[2]; in this I was showing how observational natural history was the essential, pioneering, fact-finding study which was now being converted into the quantitative science of ecology. The real goal of my lecture, however, was concerned with the relation of this new ecology to the philosophy of evolutionary studies and particularly to those concerned with the nature of man. Since the number of readers was local and small, I will quote some paragraphs from it for, although now forty years old, they will, I think, be seen to be not only relevant to the theme of our book, but

---

[2] It has long been out of print, but copies are to be found in the national copyright libraries.

15

as an introduction to it. After discussing some points about my former research in marine biology in relation to the fisheries – Aberdeen being an important fishing port – I went on as follows:

> Perhaps I may make a confession. I have worked hard at marine ecology, but I have done so only partly because I have had a desire to benefit the fishing industry; I have this desire most sincerely, but also I have felt that I have been working towards a better understanding of animal relationships and making contributions to the development of general principles in ecology . . .
>
> I will go further – I will confess that perhaps my main interest in ecology is the conviction that this science of inter-relationships of animals and their environment will eventually have a reaction for the benefit of mankind quite apart from any immediate economic one. I believe that one of the great contributions of biology in this century to the welfare of the race will be the working out of ecological principles that can be applied to human affairs; the establishment of an ecological outlook. I believe the only true science of politics is that of human ecology – a quantitative science which will take in not only the economic and nutritional needs of man, but one which will embrace his emotional side as well, including the recognition of his spiritual as well as his physical behaviour . . .

When I speak of a science of politics, I should qualify the statement by pointing out that, of course, not all politics can be reduced to a science; so much of it is burning with powerful emotions – is passionate and not a part of science. By a science of politics I here mean the systematic arrangement of the facts upon which political discussion must centre.

Here I was advocating, more than forty years ago, what might well be called a sociobiology, to use the term now

16

fashionable in the USA; there is, however, an important difference from that of Professor Edward O. Wilson who has pioneered this approach in America (see his *On Human Nature*, Harvard University Press, 1978). I am full of admiration for Wilson's thesis and the fact that he recognizes the importance in human culture of man's religious side, but as we shall see in Chapter 10 (p. 189), he attempts to relate it to an entirely materialistic biology and in this, I am sure, on the evidence to be presented later, that he must be wrong.

Let me continue with the quotation from my original Aberdeen address:

> If we look at history, that part of the evolutionary cavalcade to which we are nearest, we cannot help being struck by the fact that so many of the great movements and upheavals in human society have been idealistic ones. The wars of conflicting ideologies have been more bitter and violent than those fought for purely economic ends . . . I believe that the dogmatic assertions of the mechanistic biologists [which I had been discussing in an earlier part of the lecture] . . . are as damaging to the peace of mind of humanity as was the belief in everyday miracles in the middle ages. I believe what Professor Joad said the other day in that popular war-time radio programme, *The Brains Trust*, [I was speaking in 1942] to be profoundly true; 'that the unconsciously frustrated desire for spiritual experience is no less important than the unconsciously frustrated sex upon which the psycho-analysts have laid so much stress' . . .
>
> Plants, rooted to one spot, are certainly at the mercy of their environment; but animals which can move about have an opportunity to choose their habitat. In the evolution of motile animals there are two opposing selections at work. In the words of Mr Charles Elton, who has most forcibly brought this concept forward, there is 'the selection of the environment by the animal

17

as opposed to the natural selection of the animal by the environment'[3]

I had more to say along these lines of thought in the address I gave as president of the zoology section of the British Association for the Advancement of Science at Newcastle-upon-Tyne in 1949; I entitled it 'Zoology Outside the Laboratory'[4]. I had by then realized that the concept I was feeling for had already been put forward under the name of 'organic selection'. To explain this I will similarly quote some passages from this address of thirty-three years ago, for I believe that these too have a distinct bearing on the subject of our book. After discussing various kinds of research being conducted outside the laboratory, I continue as follows:

> A still more important contribution that field zoology can make to evolutionary theory is to throw more light on the part played by organic selection. The gene combinations which are best suited to the *habits* of the animal may tend to survive in preference to those which do not give such full scope to the animal's pattern of behaviour. This idea of organic selection, which was put forward independently by Baldwin and Lloyd Morgan at the turn of the century, had been almost forgotten until quite recently. This possible selection of structural variations by habit as opposed to the selection of other variations by the environment may indeed be a factor of importance. It is in effect similar to that postulated by Lamarck but brought about on Darwinian lines. External natural selection must of course be important, but if organic selection can be shown to be a really significant factor, it may well alter our way of looking at evolution as a whole. The relative importance of the two forms of selection must be the subject both of experiment and of more research into the habits and behaviour of animals in nature.

[3] *Animal Ecology and Evolution* (Oxford, 1930)
[4] *Advancement of Science*, 6 pp. 221–31, 1949

The study of animal behaviour is another important field being opened up by zoologists outside the laboratory, using the experimental method; it also has, I am sure, a great contribution to make to man's philosophy.

Zoology in the laboratory is apt to lead towards a mechanistic view of life if it becomes divorced from the world of living reality outside it. No one in his senses will deny that the laws of physics and chemistry hold good within the animal body as outside it and that the body is, in its *physical* make-up, a machine. If we investigate it in the laboratory by physical and chemical means we can of course only get physical and chemical answers. It is a much worn platitude to say that it is nonsense to consider the works of a Shakespeare, a Beethoven or a Rembrandt as the products of a machine; but it is a platitude worth repeating. If man is a member of the animal kingdom as we all believe, his works of genius are a manifestation of organic behaviour. To proclaim that [such] organic behaviour is the product of mechanism as we *ordinarily understand it* is to my mind as unreasonable and as dogmatic as to proclaim the literal interpretation of Genesis . . . I do not doubt that all science is one, but I do question that physics and chemistry as we know them will be found to explain the whole of science. To express what I feel I cannot do better than quote the concluding words of the presidential address which [the late] Professor Sir James Gray gave to this section in 1933:

'Experimental zoology can be divided into two types of study: (1) the investigation of the physical and chemical properties of living organisms; (2) a study of the intrinsic potentialities of living matter, revealing as it does a co-ordination of events which is without inanimate parallel. In the first type of work we must use each new weapon which the physicist can give us. In the second type of work, however, biology must be the mistress and not the servant of physics and chemistry. She must make her own foundations, and build on them fearlessly, prepared to change her views, if need be, but not prepared to force the wine of life into bottles which were designed for use in the simpler and less intoxicating fields of chemical science.'

Then, after referring to some of the ideas put forward by the late Dr E. S. Russell in his book *The Directiveness of Organic Activities* (Cambridge University Press, 1946), I went on as follows:

Let us look again at the modern view of evolution which, as far as it goes, I fully accept. Variations are selected to bring about animals better and better adapted to their way of life. Man by his selective breeding can alter the form of domestic animals to suit, within limits, his own desires; he selects those which better suit his needs. I am now going to say something which might easily be misunderstood and, perhaps, is dangerous to say. I am saying it only for the sake of argument, and not advocating something I necessarily think desirable. What I want to say is this. No modern biologist would doubt that if we knew as much about the genetics of man as we do about the genetics of some animals then, if mankind wished to control marriages by law, he could, by permitting some and prohibiting others, gradually in the course of long periods of time alter the human race. Modern biology points to that, not as something desirable or undesirable, but as a theoretical possibility. [Since I gave this address there has now come the possibility of 'genetic engineering'.] If that is in fact a logical deduction from the present biological position, you will see where it must lead us. Evolution would no longer be guided from outside the species by natural selection, but by a directive activity from within the organism itself. We would see an organism directing its own evolution towards a goal in the future, whatever that might be decided to be. If that would not be an example of organic *directiveness* then I don't know the meaning of the word.

In the hypothetical case just given, although man would be carrying out conscious organic selection, he would still be subject to natural selection by external agencies: for example, the elimination of certain gene combinations less resistant than others to the attacks of pathogenic organisms. There would be an interplay between the two selections: natural and directive. We have seen that in nature there is probably a similar interplay between natural selection from without and organic selection from within.

In 1954 I was joint editor with Sir Julian Huxley and Dr E. B. Ford of the book of essays entitled *Evolution as a Process* (George Allen and Unwin) to which I contributed 'Escape from Specialization'; then in 1974 I joined a number of colleagues in preparing the new introduction designed to bring up to date the third edition of Sir Julian Huxley's *Evolution: the Modern Synthesis*, and here I reviewed the increasing evidence for the importance of behaviour as a selective force within the Darwinian system to which I shall be referring in the present volume.

Now let me come to my own book on evolution which was the published version of my first series of Gifford Lectures delivered in the University of Aberdeen in 1964 and entitled *The Living Stream* (Collins, 1965); here is the account of evolution theory as I saw it, together with some of the ideas I would add to it which I felt would make a significant difference to the Darwinian theory. I was at first disappointed at its reception by my strictly biological colleagues. If I had wanted their attention I should have known better than to give it the sub-title; 'A restatement of evolution theory and its relation to the spirit of man'; I had hardly a word from them. I don't believe they looked at it after reading that sub-title, and I could almost hear them saying, 'Poor old Hardy's round the bend.' With the philosophers it was different.

I would here like to relate a little story. I used to enjoy, and still do, talking to undergraduate societies, but in discussion I would frequently be told, 'Oh, I don't think Popper would agree with you there'; I had read a lot of Sir Karl Popper's work and didn't really feel we were at odds with one another. Yet such remarks would continue to be made and I began to think of him as a kind of bogey-man I couldn't understand. The reader can imagine my delight when I received from Sir Karl a copy of his famous lecture, 'Of Clouds and Clocks: an Approach to the Problem of Rationality and the Freedom of Man' inscribed to me in these words: 'With the expression of the greatest admiration for *The Living Stream*'. Few intellectual events in my life have pleased me more.

My second series of Gifford Lectures was entitled *The Divine Flame* (Collins, 1966) with the sub-title 'An Essay towards a Natural History of Religion'; in this I proposed the setting up of a research unit to study personal accounts of religious experience. Had I not become so engrossed in the results of this work I might have tried to bring out a new edition of *The Living Stream*.

It is the results of these latter researches, which have been brought together in my last book, *The Spiritual Nature of Man* (Oxford University Press, 1979), that make me all the more convinced that the Darwinian doctrine must be enlarged in such a way that it is no longer at odds with man's spiritual experience. To explain the nature of this change is the purpose of this book. Whilst it will contain some of the material that was in *The Living Stream*, including some of the drawings and diagrams, it must not be thought of as just a new edition of that work, for it goes much further; it will also touch on some of the ideas to be found in another of my books, *The Biology of God* (Cape, 1975). The present book develops my thoughts on the subject of its title over many years, together with a brief account of the results of the researches into religious experience to which I have just referred. I can only hope that I have brought them together into a unified whole, for that, indeed, is what I believe them to be.

What I have written here I hope may be to some extent a contribution towards the resolving of what I can only regard as an intellectual scandal of the academic world of today. No one could have greater admiration than I have for the marvellous work and discoveries of the contemporary molecular biologists, but to suppose that this is the whole explanation of *life* is nonsense. We cannot have it both ways. We must, as I hope to convince you, regard man as the product of a long evolutionary process; yet equally no one in his senses can really believe that the great works of art, in literature, painting or music, or the love of natural beauty, are the result of physico-chemical reactions as we know them today. This applies even more to what I am calling the spiritual awareness of man, to be discussed later in the book.

2

The Reality of Evolution

Charles Darwin was not, of course, the originator of the idea of evolution, but with his book *The Origin of Species*, published in 1859, he was indeed the first to convince the greater part of the intellectual world of its reality.

He carried conviction not only because he had a remarkable genius for the marshalling of the facts both of his own natural history observations and those of others, but he put forward the first reasonable explanation as to how evolution comes about: the principle he called natural selection. This theory was, as is well-known and will be recalled in the next chapter, independently put forward in 1858 by Alfred Russel Wallace; there is, however, irrefutable evidence, as we shall see, that Darwin had written an account of his theory at least fourteen years before this. I shall be dealing at length with the nature and power of natural selection later in the book; in this chapter I hope to convince the reader, if he had had any doubts about it, of the reality of the process of evolution without considering at all the actual causes underlying it.

Darwin's early ideas as to the possibility of evolution undoubtedly came to him as a naturalist on his famous five years' voyage round the world on the surveying ship HMS *Beagle* (27 December 1831 to 2 October 1836). It was not only, however, his observations as a naturalist which were so important, and important they certainly were, but also his reading on the voyage Charles Lyell's great book *Principles of Geology* which had come out shortly before he sailed; he had taken it with him on the advice of his friend Professor Henslow who, it is amusing to recall, told Darwin in recom-

mending it as interesting reading 'to take no notice of his theories'. It was certainly Lyell's theories that had a profound influence on Darwin's thoughts; perhaps they may have had a greater effect on him than he himself actually realized, as I think we shall see.

Lyell's great merit was that he brought the geologists back to the pioneer views of Hutton (1736–97), who is often called the father of modern geology, and developed them much further. Hutton had been not only the first to demonstrate the volcanic origin of many rocks but also showed the effects of erosion, the carving out of valleys by rivers and the action of the sea; he showed the history of the earth to be a continuous natural process. These views had come in for strong criticism by the so-called 'catastrophists' who then ruled the day and believed the history of the world had been dominated by a series of catastrophies of which Noah's flood was considered to be the most recent. Lyell convinced the geologists that Hutton had been right and that the formation of the various layers of the rocks forming the earth's crust was indeed due to a succession of natural causes. Certainly Darwin was impressed and the realization of this long continuous process in the history of the earth prepared the way for his future thoughts on a continuous process of evolution; it is possible, however, that Lyell's book had an even more direct effect.

Many people have supposed that Lyell was not an evolutionist until he read Darwin's account of his theory; this, however, was not so, as was clearly indicated in Professor Judd's delightful little book *The Coming of Evolution* (Cambridge University Press, 1910). In Lyell's *Life and Letters* we see that whilst Darwin was still away on the *Beagle* he wrote to John Herschel in 1836 as follows:

In regard to the origination of new species, I am very glad to find that you think it probable that it may be carried on through the intervention of intermediate causes. I left this rather to be inferred, not thinking it

mending it as interesting reading 'to take no notice of his theories'. It was certainly Lyell's theories that had a profound influence on Darwin's thoughts; perhaps they may have had a greater effect on him than he himself actually realized, as I think we shall see.

Lyell's great merit was that he brought the geologists back to the pioneer views of Hutton (1736–97), who is often called the father of modern geology, and developed them much further. Hutton had been not only the first to demonstrate the volcanic origin of many rocks but also showed the effects of erosion, the carving out of valleys by rivers and the action of the sea; he showed the history of the earth to be a continuous natural process. These views had come in for strong criticism by the so-called 'catastrophists' who then ruled the day and believed the history of the world had been dominated by a series of catastrophies of which Noah's flood was considered to be the most recent. Lyell convinced the geologists that Hutton had been right and that the formation of the various layers of the rocks forming the earth's crust was indeed due to a succession of natural causes. Certainly Darwin was impressed and the realization of this long continuous process in the history of the earth prepared the way for his future thoughts on a continuous process of evolution; it is possible, however, that Lyell's book had an even more direct effect.

Many people have supposed that Lyell was not an evolutionist until he read Darwin's account of his theory; this, however, was not so, as was clearly indicated in Professor Judd's delightful little book *The Coming of Evolution* (Cambridge University Press, 1910). In Lyell's *Life and Letters* we see that whilst Darwin was still away on the *Beagle* he wrote to John Herschel in 1836 as follows:

In regard to the origination of new species, I am very glad to find that you think it probable that it may be carried on through the intervention of intermediate causes. I left this rather to be inferred, not thinking it their heads and kicking their food into their mouths by their legs', but this is not strictly true; the reality is much more interesting for their legs, fringed with these hair-like cirri, together form a net which rhythmically sweeps from the water the finest plankton upon which they feed. I have written at greater length than perhaps I need have done to illustrate the evolutionary significance of the larval stages of these remarkable animals, but I have done so partly for another purpose; Darwin had become specially interested in barnacles after discovering several new kinds during the voyage of the *Beagle* and in addition to all his work on evolution he began in 1846 an eight-year study for a great monograph, *The Cirripedia*, published in two thick volumes in 1855.

The fourth line of evidence is that of the geographical distribution of animals and plants and no better example could be taken than that already mentioned of Darwin finding that the birds and reptiles of the various islands of the Galapagos group differed from one another and from those of the mainland; this suggesting they had undergone gradual changes as they had been separated from one another in different types of habitat. This is just a small example of a multitude of others on a vastly greater scale as we consider the differences between the fauna and flora of whole continental systems. I shall have more to say about Darwin and the Galapagos Islands in the next chapter (p. 56).

The four different kinds of observation just discussed, although strongly suggesting descent from common ancestors, are all examples of circumstantial evidence. The fifth kind is of quite a different nature and will form the main subject of this chapter. It is the evidence from palaeontology, the study of the record of past forms of life preserved for us as fossil remains in the sedementary rocks laid down over vast periods of time; they range from the Cambrian period, dated with reasonable certainty as beginning some 500 million years ago, to the most recent fossil-bearing rocks. Over this vast period of time we see the actual record of thousands of different lines of animal and plant life gradually changing in their nature with the passage of time; some appear to branch out into several new lines, others come to an end in extinction. There are gaps in the records; during some periods the lines are far more complete than in others, and with the extended work of the palaeontologists the gaps are continually being filled in. When one thinks of the precarious nature of just the right conditions for fossil formation, the wonder surely is that we have so complete a record as we do.

It is quite clear that life has been developing in the world over a vastly longer period than that of which we have any record; before the Cambrian the rocks are so old and have undergone such changes that it is very difficult to get a good idea of the life of those far-off times from such fossils as have been preserved for us, but in the Cambrian period itself we have the fossil remains of nearly all the major animal groups except the vertebrates which appear later. Here, 500 million years ago, are representatives of the crustaceans, the molluscs, the brachiopods (lamp shells), echinoderms (sea-urchin-like animals), segmented worms and other kinds of invertebrate life well recognized by zoologists as being of the same general kind as their more modern representatives of today. The existence of these remains of well recognized types of considerable complexity of structure already in existence so many millions of years ago, shows us that life of some kind must have been in existence for at least some 1,500 million years before that.

The sequence of fossils presents us with an actual factual record of the changes that have come about in the structure of the members of these long lines of animals belonging to different classificatory groups. Whilst they don't tell us anything about the causes of their evolution, they do show us that a process of change did actually take place in every one of the thousands of lines of succession presented to us if there are a sufficient number of fossils available from the different rocks to show a reasonably good sequence. Within the groups of vertebrate animals which leave us the best fossil records of their skeletons of bone, we can draw series of *time* charts of these changes which are every bit as real as the *spatial* maps of geographical features in an atlas. Here we see the facts of evolutionary change clearly recorded. In this chapter I am presenting just such a time atlas of charts redrawn and slightly re-arranged from those of the late Professor Alfred S. Romer given in his book *Vertebrate Palaeontology* which I also used with his kind permission in my former book *The Living Stream*.

In different periods of the earth's history we see some

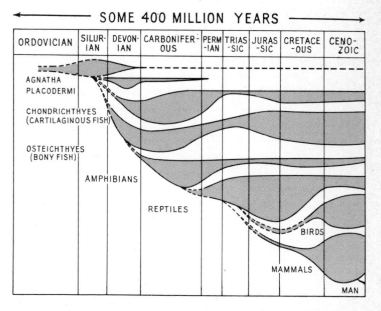

SOME 400 MILLION YEARS

1. A graphic representation of the origin and relative success of the main vertebrate groups with the passage of time since the Ordovician period of some 400 million years ago. The comparative abundance of the different groups is roughly indicated by the thickness of the bands. Redrawn and slightly rearranged from a chart by Professor Alfred S. Romer in his *Vertebrate Palaeontology*.

Taken from the author's work *The Living Stream* (Collins, 1965), p. 21.

groups of animals being more successful than others, some waxing, others waning and some dying out altogether. The varying widths of the bands in the charts representing the different groups indicate their relative success measured not in actual numbers of individuals found but in the number of different species of that type of animal in the succession of geological periods from the past to the present day. The first chart, fig. 1, shows in broad outline the succession of the main classes of vertebrate animals over the last 400 million

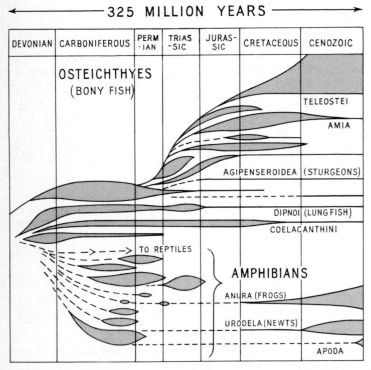

2. The evolution of the main groups of bony fish and amphibians arranged similarly to fig. 1 and also redrawn from Romer. Note the arrow marked 'to reptiles' among the most primitive amphibians; at this point should be added the chart in fig. 3.
From *The Living Stream*, p. 22.

years from the primitive fish-like creatures to the later amphibians which began the conquest of the land, to the reptiles which completed the conquest and on to the birds and mammals. The existence of evolutionary change cannot be denied. We also see the approximate points of origin of one group from another and here we notice the interesting fact that the new groups tend to arise from the *earlier* representatives of the preceding ones; later on in their history the members of any group tend to become more and more specialized for their life in different habitats and so less likely to give rise to new types which may mark the beginning of a new line – a new class – of animals.

Fig. 2 shows us the time chart of the evolution of the bony fish, or Osteichthyes to use their scientific classificatory name, and also the early amphibians of which so many became extinct in the Permian and Triassic periods. The bony fish were a very successful group giving rise to the enormous number of different kinds of teleost fish we have throughout the world today. The origin of the modern amphibians: the frogs and toads, the many different newt-like animals and those curious burrowing creatures, the Apoda, which as their name implies have lost their legs and lead a worm-like existence in the soil.

The reptiles which, as we have said, completed the conquest of the land arose in the far-off Carboniferous age from early amphibians; here the record of their origin is not yet well represented but palaeontologists have no doubt that it is just a matter of time before the fossils that will show this origin are discovered. However, once the early reptiles appeared on the land in the late Carboniferous some 200 million years ago we see how their stock radiated out in so many different directions as its members were able to colonize quite new kinds of environment. Wherever they found unoccupied territory that would give them a living they at once moved in, driven forward by the competition for food and space. These sudden outbursts in evolution into so many different new kinds are known by the term adaptive radiation which well describes them. This is well shown in Romer's time chart reproduced (in modified form) in fig. 3. Here he has, for economy of space, lumped together a mass of different forms, which could have been represented by separate lines, under the general name of the archosaurian orders; they include the many different kinds of dinosaurs, the flying pterodactyls, the ancestors of the crocodiles and many more which if space had allowed them to be shown separately would have greatly enhanced the effect of this explosion of new types.

We shall see the same great outburst of new forms as the mammals take over from the reptiles which had so suddenly died out during or at the end of the Cretaceous period. Opinion is still very divided as to the cause of this great decline of the reptiles; was it due to the effects of some extra-terrestrial occurrence, such as the earth being hit by a giant meteorite which temporarily led to an almost world-wide destruction of vegetation on account of harmful chemicals being spread through the earth's atmosphere? There have been many other ideas; we must just note its occurrence and the tremendous effect it had on the future of vertebrate evolution as the mammals replaced the reptiles. In chart 4, we see twenty-two distinct orders of mammals (including nine which are now extinct) all coming into existence in the Paleocene period. In the chart the different orders are given their scientific names; along the righthand margin, however, I have placed numbers which refer to the common names of the members of the different groups given in the legend below the figure. It is these sudden and rapid increases in the rate at which evolution has taken place which has caused some geologists to doubt that natural selection can have been the real cause of the changes. We certainly see how different may be the speed of such change in these different geological periods. Once the Chiroptera – the bats – have become winged aerial creatures in the early Eocene they remain bats for the rest of the time to the present day; similarly with carnivores, the artiodactyls (sheep, oxen, deer, antelopes,

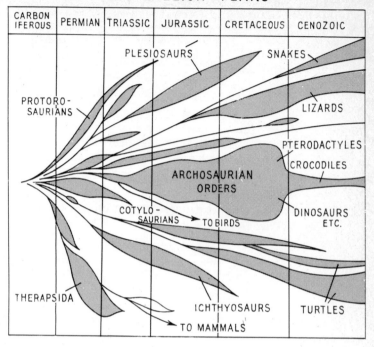

3. The evolution of the main groups of reptiles arranged as in former figures and again redrawn from Romer. The archosaurian orders (crocodiles, pterodactyles, dinosaurs, etc.) have been massed together in one band for simplicity; they should be represented by eight separate diverging lines (shown by Romer in another chart) each as important as the other main lines shown here and each, except for the crocodiles, becoming extinct at the end of the Cretaceous period. The thin line reaching the present day, between the bands representing the lizards and the crocodiles, is for *Sphenodon punctatus*, the tuatara, the single representative of an ancient mesozoic group of reptiles, lingering on in isolation on some small islands off New Zealand. Note the arrows showing the points of origin of the birds and mammals; the latter leads on to fig. 4. From *The Living Stream*, p. 23.

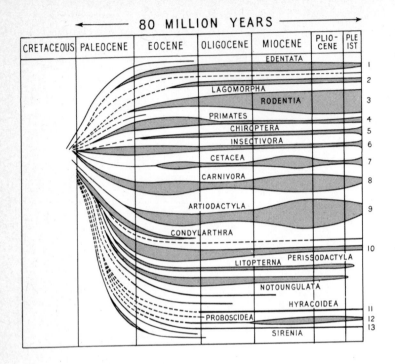

<- 80 MILLION YEARS ->

| CRETACEOUS | PALEOCENE | EOCENE | OLIGOCENE | MIOCENE | PLIO-CENE | PLE-IST |

EDENTATA — 1
2
LAGOMORPHA
RODENTIA — 3
PRIMATES — 4
CHIROPTERA — 5
INSECTIVORA — 6
CETACEA — 7
CARNIVORA — 8
ARTIODACTYLA — 9
CONDYLARTHRA
10
LITOPTERNA PERISSODACTYLA
NOTOUNGULATA
HYRACOIDEA — 11
PROBOSCIDEA — 12
SIRENIA — 13

4. The history of the different orders of the placental mammals showing their remarkably rapid radiation in the early Paleocene; also redrawn from Romer. The common names of the main representatives of the different orders, which are referred to by the numbers on the right of the chart, are as follows: (1) anteaters, sloths and armadillos; (2) hares and rabbits; (3) rats, mice and other rodents; (4) lemurs, monkeys, apes and man; (5) bats; (6) shrews, moles, hedgehogs, etc.; (7) whales, dolphins and porpoises; (8) cats, dogs, bears, seals, etc.; (9) oxen, sheep, deer, antelopes, camels, etc.; (10) rhinoceroses, tapirs and horses; (11) the hyrax (or rock coney); (12) elephants; (13) sea-cows: the manatee and the dugong.
From *The Living Stream*, p. 24.

36

etc.), insectivores and other groups which, once they have made the fundamental adaptive change fitting them for their particular kind of life, undergo no major alterations in their characteristic structure except greater and greater specialization to different kinds of habitat and different types of behaviour. These changes in the rate of evolution need not cause the geologists to doubt the working of Darwinian selection. The small changes due to gene mutations do not become more frequent, nor do they become larger; as group

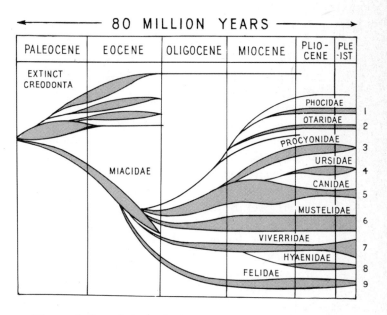

5. The evolution of the main families of just one of the orders of placental mammals: the Carnivora. Note the radiation of the modern forms replacing the more primitive creodonts which became extinct at the end of the Eocene. The common names of the typical members of the families, referred to by the numbers at the right of the figure, are as follows: (1) seals; (2) sealions; (3) racoons and pandas; (4) bears; (5) dogs; (6) weasels, martens, otters, skunks; (7) civets; (8) hyenas; and (9) cats.
From *The Living Stream*, p. 25.

after group is presented with new ecological niches to occupy, their rate of adaptational change, through natural selection, is greatly increased in the early stages of exploiting these new empty habitats.

I will give one more chart from Alfred Romer's series, that in fig. 5, where he has taken us into greater detail to show how in any one of these orders of mammals we can see just the same kind of splitting up into separate lesser groups – the classificatory 'families'; in this example he has chosen the order Carnivora, the flesh-eating mammals which may be divided into the families of cats, dogs, hyenas, bears, seals, sea-lions and so on. Here we see an interesting point in that all the modern carnivores did not come into being until a group of quite considerable size, the primitive creodont carnivores had flourished and become practically extinct at the end of the Eocene period; once again we see a rapid adaptive radiation of the modern carnivores to take the places left by the creodonts which were either driven out by competition with the more modern and efficient forms or became extinct for other reasons.

The charts I have just shown present us with the factual records of the sequence of the different forms of vertebrate life on the earth over the last some 400 million years; they do not tell us how this long series of changes has taken place – that will come later. No one, I think, can reasonably doubt that here we have a true representation of the actual evolutionary process among the vertebrate animals. There are available many such series of charts showing similar evolutionary changes among the various invertebrate animals such as the molluscs of different classes, the echinoderms (the sea-urchin and starfish-like animals), the crustaceans including the great group of the now extinct trilobites, also the extinct marine scorpions and many other major groups.

My next illustration (fig. 6) is not factual, but an entirely imaginary diagram to show how the individual species in the different genera might be represented in a similar time chart. The problem of how new species are actually formed will be

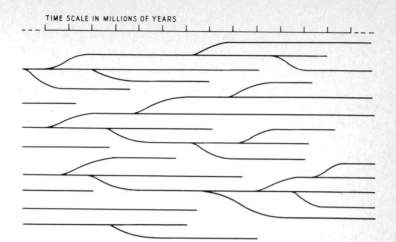

6. A diagram to show the typical evolution of the separate species within several different genera where sufficient fossils are available to trace them back to common ancestors. Each line represents the continuing *whole population* of a single species with the passage of time; many such lines are seen to end in extinction. Each well defined branching group of species may be regarded as a genus, and several such related genera are classed together as a family.
From *The Living Stream*, p. 26.

dealt with in a separate chapter later in the book (p. 82); it is at first surprising to realize how very recently it is that we have fully understood this process. My diagram shows new species branching off and becoming established, whilst others die out. Here I want to consider this pattern of evolution a little more fully without, as I have said, going into the actual causes of the process.

I gave my former book its title, *The Living Stream*, because the process of evolution as we see it reminded me of a river of life, but, as I said when I coined the phrase, it is a river *flowing in reverse*; a real river is of course always running downhill and each such stream is being fed by tributaries as it proceeds on its course. In my diagram in fig. 6, if for a moment we take no notice of the time scale along the top, we could say that it might well represent a series of streams or little river systems all flowing from right to left and each one being fed by small tributaries which join it on its way to the sea far off to the left of the figure. Now take note of the time scale along the top and our streams of life are seen to be flowing in the *opposite* direction, from left to right. The little branches, here representing individual species, seem *at first sight* to look very like the branches seen in charts 1 to 5 which being the larger groups – classes, orders and families – are radically different from the small branches of the species. In our understanding of evolution it is essential that this difference is understood, but I'm afraid I cannot reveal the true nature of the species until we have discussed the mechanism of the evolutionary process; the species is a unique category of life. I have introduced this diagram to follow the series of geological charts for quite a different reason – to show that this living stream is indeed like a river running in reverse, for we can see it running uphill!

In the Carboniferous period we see the amphibia rising out of the water to have a partial existence on the land and then the reptiles completing the conquest. Now if we look at the great array of terrestrial vertebrates we will see some of them coming to live in the highest mountains, some like the birds, bats and extinct pterodactyls taking to flight with many of the birds migrating for thousands of miles. The stream of life may indeed flow uphill.

As I have already said, the animal body is a physico-chemical machine, without implying that that is all it is; it is an engine – a vehicle carrying life – driven by the fuel of food and so can overcome the force of gravity. In *The Living Stream* I have gone into this matter in more detail and discussed it in relation to the second law of thermodynamics and the views of other scientists, notably the great physicist, the late Professor Edwin Schrödinger, who in his book *What is Life?* (1944) had much to say on this matter.

I have sometimes thought that perhaps a better simile to that of the living stream being like a river system in reverse would be that of an incoming tide. Who has not watched the tide rising over an esturine mud-flat and seen the little streams of water dividing out to fill first one little gully in the mud's surface and then another? The stream is rising, being driven over the surface by the inexorable force of the moon's gravitational attraction; the stream of life is being driven forward and into every available space that will take it by the tremendous reproductive pressure to which all forms of life are subjected.

Nearly all animals and plants, except some of the most primitive, have a sexual form of reproduction, but those which do not, and reproduce simply by dividing into two, will present a very different picture of the course of their evolution from that of sexually breeding organisms. Diagrammatically such a non-sexual form of evolution would look like that shown in fig. 7 as a simple repetition of a process of

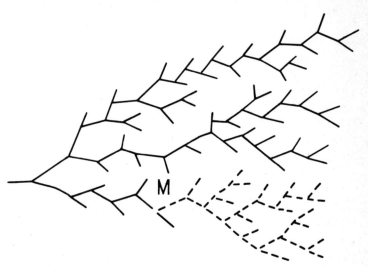

7. Evolution in a non-sexual organism which reproduces by budding or by dividing in two; the species goes on multiplying with no genetical change until a mutation occurs at M and gives rise to a new strain (shown in broken line).
From *The Living Stream*, p. 36.

dividing into two; if some mutational change takes place, as at M in the diagram, where a new variety is formed, then a new branch of a slightly different type of organism will appear and enter into competition with the older more typical kind. It is surprising that many people seem to think of the process of general evolution as being like this, only, on account of sex, being just a little more complicated; the fact is that sex completely alters the whole process.

I now show in fig. 8 a diagram I made for *The Living Stream* to help our consideration of the nature of the process. Along the top of the diagram is a scale of past generations; towards the right is that of the present day marked by an arrow pointing downwards towards a series of circles each representing individual members of the population. Only one individual in the present generation, and the genetic streams leading up to him (or her) from the past and then on to the future, are shown in solid line; other such streams are shown in broken line. As we go back to the generations of the past – to our parents, grandparents, great grandparents and so on – we see how thick on the ground, so to speak, our forebears become; now going in the other direction from a present-day individual towards the future, to the right, we see radiating genetic lines fusing with those from other individuals to form the generations to come. This, I believe, is the real representation of the living stream and in thinking about the mechanism of evolution, as we shall begin to do in the next and later chapters, we should not forget it.

Just as so many people in the past have thought that the introduction of sexual reproduction merely complicates the process without fundamentally changing it, so do many people seem to think that evolution can for simplicity be thought of as lines of individuals slightly altering from time to time and branching to give new lines. As my diagram should show, we are dealing not with lines of individuals but with vast populations. It is populations which are gradually changing in the process of evolution and we must realize, as we shall when we have discussed the mechanism of the

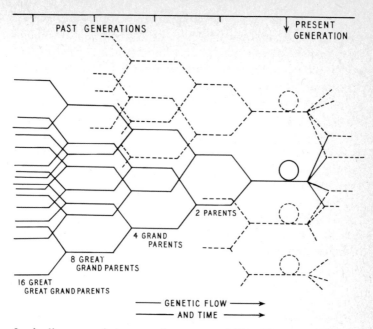

2 PARENTS

4 GRAND PARENTS

8 GREAT GRAND PARENTS

16 GREAT GREAT GRAND PARENTS

GENETIC FLOW ⟶
AND TIME ⟶

8. A diagram of the genetic stream of life. The horizontal un-broken line with a circle attached represents *one* individual of a population at the present time; the lines linked to it coming from the left represent its past ancestral individuals and the radiating lines to the right, joining with the lines from the other individuals (shown in *broken* line) represent the reproductive cells fusing to form the coming new generation to the right. If we consider a population of millions, many having common ancestors, we may imagine the true complexity of the stream.
From *The Living Stream*, p. 38.

process a little more, that no two individuals in the population are exactly the same, except in the rare cases of identical twins, which are the result of a reproductive accident.

H. G. Wells, in one of his sociological studies, surprised the reader by asking the question, 'Have you ever thought how many direct ancestors you might have had say at the time of the Norman Conquest?' If we allow some thirty years to represent a generation it would be some thirty generations back to 1066, some 900 years ago. We have, of course, two parents, four grandparents, eight great grandparents and so on; I now reproduce a statistical table which I gave in *The Living Stream* to show that if we (and other members of the population) did not have the same ancestors again and again in our past history, going back thirty generations, we should each have had over a *thousand million* ancestors living at the time of the Norman Conquest! We are told, however, that at the time of Queen Anne the population of the whole of Great Britain was only about five million and that at the time of the Norman Conquest it was probably much less. What does it mean? It can only mean that more often than not we have all shared the same ancestors many times. It means in fact that most of you, my readers, are likely to be more closely related to one another than you had ever suspected.

TABLE I

Generations back	Ancestors	Generations back	Ancestors
1	2	16	65,536
2	4	17	131,072
3	8	18	262,144
4	16	19	524,288
5	32	20	1,048,576
6	64	21	2,097,152
7	128	22	4,194,304
8	256	23	8,388,608
9	512	24	16,777,216
10	1,024	25	33,554,432
11	2,048	26	67,108,864
12	4,096	27	134,217,728
13	8,192	28	268,435,456
14	16,384	29	536,870,912
15	32,768	30	1,073,741,824

Such indeed is the complexity of the populations which are evolving and the nature of which we must consider – populations stretching back over some 2,000 million years. Within this stream the little genetic currents continually meet and split apart again, and at each meeting and splitting the genetic material is shuffled into new arrangements giving new variations; we individuals are the little eddies at these junctions. Is that all that we are? That is the question we are about to explore.

3

The Greatness
of Darwin and Wallace

As I have already recalled Darwin was by no means the first to suggest that a continuous evolution of living beings had taken place. The idea dates back to Lucretius and classical times, and then in the Renaissance it was the philosophers Spinoza and Leibnitz who mentioned the possibility before the scientists did; in 1790 Kant in his *Kritik der Urtheilskraft* wrote (and I use the translation of J. H. Bernard) concerning the diversity of vertebrate animals: 'This analogy of forms, which with all the differences seem to have been produced according to a common original type, strengthens our suspicions of an actual relationship between them in their production from a common parent.'[1]

First among the scientists I will take that remarkable French mathematician and physicist Louis Moreau de Maupertuis (1698–1759) who in 1745 in his *Venus Physique* put forward what I believe is the very earliest genetical theory to explain 'the production of accidental varieties and the succession of those varieties from one generation to another, and finally the establishment or destruction of species'. In 1751 he further enlarged and generalized this theory in his *Système de la Nature* to account for the origin of all existing species. Now here come two remarkable examples of a foreshadowing of the ideas of Charles Darwin himself. The first is the less important, but interesting in its similarity to

[1] In *The Living Stream* (Collins, 1965) pp. 41–61, I review this early history.

46

the idea which Darwin suggested over a hundred years later towards the end of his *Variation of Animals and Plants under Domestication* (1868) and called his hypothesis of pangenesis, but I will not go into this here, for it is the second point which is much the more surprising; in his *Essai de Cosmologie*, Maupertuis actually anticipated the theory of natural selection: 'In the fortuitous combination of the products of nature . . .' he wrote, 'only those with certain adaptive relationships could survive . . . in the other, infinitely greater part, there was neither adaptation nor order. All those have perished . . . and the species we see today are only the smallest part of those which a blind destiny produced.' I am afraid this is the merest sketch of Maupertuis's ideas; for my knowledge of him I am much indebted to Dr A. C. Crombie, Lecturer in the History of Science at Oxford.'[2]

I should just mention Buffon (1707–88) who first indicated his belief in evolutionary change in the 1755 edition of his *Histoire Naturelle* where he attributed it to the *direct* influence of the environment, an idea, as I shall show later (p. 51), that has so often been wrongly associated with Lamarck.

We come now to that great character, Dr Erasmus Darwin (1731–1802, the grandfather of Charles) who became one of the leaders of intellectual life in England towards the end of the eighteenth century, and put forward most explicit evolutionary views in his massive two-volume *Zoönomia or the Laws of Organic Life* in 1794. It was a pity that he buried them among so much other material mainly of a medical nature, for we only get to them on page 504 of his first volume. I will now give some extracts from the second (corrected) edition of 1796 (pp. 504–9):

When we revolve in our minds, first, the great changes, which we see naturally produced in animals after their nativity, as in the production of the butterfly with

[2] See his excellent 'The Idea of Organic Evolution' in *Discovery*, March 1953.

painted wings from the crawling caterpillar; or of the respiring frog from the subnatant tadpole . . .

Secondly, when we think over the great changes introduced into various animals by artificial or accidental cultivation, as in horses, which we have exercised for the different purposes of strength or swiftness, in carrying burthens or in running races; or in dogs, which have been cultivated for strength and courage, as the bulldog . . . [then, after considering a number of other points, he continues] . . .

Thirdly, when we enumerate the great changes produced in the species of animals before their nativity; these are such as resemble the form or colour of their parents, which have been altered by the cultivation or accidents above related, and are thus continued to their posterity . . .

Fourthly, when we revolve in our minds the great similarity of structures, which obtains in all the warm-blooded animals, as well as quadrupeds, birds, and amphibious animals, as in mankind; from the mouse and bat to the elephant and whale; one is led to conclude that they have alike been produced from a similar living filament . . .

In his fifth paragraph, where he speaks of a perpetual transformation of animals (i.e. evolution) 'produced by their own exertions in consequence of their desires and aversions, of their pleasures and their pains', Erasmus Darwin is forestalling by fifteen years the doctrine of Lamarck. On the next page he has a remarkable passage foreshadowing part of his grandson's doctrine of sexual selection:

A great want of one part of the animal world has consisted in the desire of the exclusive possession of the females; and these have acquired weapons to combat each other for this purpose . . . So the horns of the stag are sharp to offend his adversary, but are branched for the purpose of parrying or receiving the thrusts of horns similar to his own, and have therefore been formed for the purpose of combating other stags for the exclusive possession of the females; who are observed, like the ladies in the times of chivalry, to attend the car of the victor.

He proceeds (on p. 509) to a magnificent vision of evolution as a whole:

> Would it be too bold to imagine that in the great length of time since the earth began to exist, perhaps millions of ages before the commencement of the history of mankind, would it be too bold to imagine, that all warm-blooded animals have arisen from one living filament, which THE GREAT FIRST CAUSE endued with animality, with the power of acquiring new parts, attended with new propensities . . . and thus possessing the faculty of continuing to improve by its own inherent activity, and of delivering down those improvements by generation to its posterity, world without end!

How much did Charles Darwin get, consciously or subconsciously from his grandfather's *Zoönomia*? That is certainly a puzzle to which we shall return a little later (p. 53).

We must now turn back again to France to look at the theories of Lamarck (1744–1829), and we must at once ask ourselves a similar question as to whether he was influenced by the *Zoönomia*? The book was certainly widely read by scientists and philosophers, but I do not know of any record of Lamarck having read it; if he had, as we have just seen, he would have come across, in the briefest outline, the essence of the doctrine he was to publish himself a few years later. Lamarck first put forward his evolutionary views in his *Philosophie Zoologique* in 1809 when he enunciated two laws; I quote them from the translation of Hugh Elliot (Macmillan, 1914).

FIRST LAW

In every animal which has not passed the limit of its development, a more frequent and continuous use of any organ gradually strengthens, develops and enlarges that organ, and gives it a power proportional to the length of time it has been so used; while the permanent disuse of any organ imperceptibly weakens and deteriorates it, and progressively diminishes its functional capacity, until it finally disappears.

SECOND LAW

All the acquisitions or losses wrought by nature on individuals through the influence of the environment in which their race has long been placed, and hence through the influence of the predominant use or permanent disuse of any organ; all these are preserved by reproduction to the new individuals which arise, provided that the acquired modifications are common to both sexes, or at least to the individuals which produce the young.

Whilst we know now that Lamarck's suggested mechanism for bringing about structural change by the inherited effects of the use of some parts of the body and the disuse of others has been disproved, there are some misunderstandings about his theory which I should like to clear up here, for I shall want to refer back to them later in the book. For one thing he emphasizes the importance of changes in the animals' habits or behaviour in bringing about differences in the ways in which animals use different parts of their bodies. Then he often speaks about these changes in habits or behaviour being brought about through changes in the environment. So often writers have misrepresented him by supposing that he believed in the direct effect of the environment. He only believed in this in regard to plants and the very lowest animals; for the majority of animals he definitely denies it.

For him the real cause of evolutionary change springs from the animal's behaviour. It was Buffon, as we have just seen, who believed in the direct effect of the environment, *not* Lamarck.

Many experiments have been done with animals subjected to the direct effects of a different environment supposedly to try to show whether Lamarck was right in his views, when actually he categorically denied such effects. Let me give another quotation from Elliot's translation of the *Philosophie Zoologique*, Chap. 7, (his p. 107) where Lamarck is discussing the influence of changes in the environment on animals; he writes thus:

> I must now explain what I mean by this statement: *the environment affects the shape and organization of animals*, that is to say that when the environment becomes very different, it produces in course of time corresponding modifications in the shape and organization of animals.
>
> It is true that if this statement were to be taken literally, I should be convicted of an error; for whatever the environment may do, it does not work any direct modification whatever in the shape and organization of animals.
>
> But great alterations in the environment of animals lead to great alterations in their needs, and these alterations in their needs necessarily lead to others in their activities. Now if the new needs become permanent, the animals then adopt new habits which last as long as the needs that evoke them. This is easy to demonstrate, and indeed requires no amplification.

So important is this statement for a proper understanding of Lamarck's views that I think it may be well to give in a footnote the same passage in his original French.[3]

[3] From Chap. VII of Lamarck's *Philosophie Zoologique* Vol. I, p. 221, Paris 1809:

Ici, il devient uécessaire de m'expliquer sur le sens que j'attache à ces expressions: *Les circonstances influent sur la forme et l'organisation des*

One more point I should make regarding this pre-Darwinian period concerns the great comparative anatomist, Cuvier (1769–1832) who from his position in Paris dominated European zoology for so long; he was *not* an evolutionist and bitterly opposed Lamarck's doctrines, insisting not only on the fixity of species, but also of varieties. 'All the beings belonging to one of these forms' he said, 'perpetuated since the beginning of all things, that is the creation, constitute what we call a species.' Cuvier on the continent, and Owen in England, were the great brakes on the development of evolutionary thought.

At first sight, looking back from today, it does seem extraordinary that the ideas of Charles Darwin did not follow directly from the outburst of interest in the possibility of evolution at the end of the eighteenth and the beginning of the nineteenth centuries. So completely, however, had Cuvier stifled these earlier ideas, that when Darwin came to consider the possibility of evolutionary change he began quite afresh; there can be little doubt, I think, that he had been led to believe that these early ideas had been completely dismissed as idle speculation. He had been accused, by Samuel Butler[4] and more recently by Darlington,[5] of taking

---

animaux, c'est-à-dire qu'en devenant très-différentes, elles changent, avec le temps, et cette forme et l'organisation elle-même par des modifications proportionnées.

Assurément, si l'on prenait ces expressions à la lettre, on m'attribuerait une erreur; car quelles que puissent être les circonstances, elles n'opèrent directement sur la forme et sur l'organisation des animaux aucune modification quelconque.

Mais de grands changements dans les circonstances amènent pour les animaux de grands changements dans leurs besoins, et de pareils changements dans les besoins en amènent nécessairement dans les actions. Or, si les nouveaux besoins deviennent constants ou très-durables, les animaux prennent alors de nouvelles *habitudes*, qui sont aussi durables que les besoins qui les ont fait naître. Voilà ce qu'il est facile de démontrer, et même ce qui n'exige aucune explication pour être senti.

[4] Samuel Butler: *Evolution, Old and New*, London, 1879.
[5] C. D. Darlington: *loc. cit.*

his ideas, without acknowledgement, from his grandfather Erasmus Darwin and keeping him in the background. I cannot believe this is true. Charles, as a young man, read his grandfather's *Zoönomia*, but thought how speculative it was; he hated speculation unless it was supported by a large array of facts. He did not hurry to publish his own views; he kept on waiting, for over twenty years, for more and more evidence, and in the end was forced to publish them, as we shall see, before he was actually ready to do so. That is not the behaviour of a man who steals his ancestor's ideas to gain personal fame; and his own views except for that small part of his sexual selection theory, were entirely different from his grandfather's.

Darwin tells us in his autobiography[6] how as a student at Edinburgh – and he went there at the age of sixteen in 1825 – he met Grant who later became Professor of Zoology at University College, London. After saying Grant was his senior by several years, he writes:

> He one day, when we were walking together, burst forth in high admiration of Lamarck and his views on evolution. I listened in silent astonishment and, as far as I can judge, without any effect on my mind. I had previously read the *Zoönomia* of my grandfather, in which similar views are maintained, but without producing any effect on me. Nevertheless it is probable that the hearing rather early in life such views maintained and praised may have favoured my upholding them under a different form in my *Origin of Species*. At this time I admired greatly the *Zoönomia*; but on reading it a second time after an interval of ten or fifteen years, I was much disappointed, the proportion of speculation being so large to the facts given.

I cannot help smiling at this last remark, for could anything be more speculative and lacking in factual support than his

[6] On p. 49 of the complete version edited by Nora Barlow, London, 1958.

own theory of pan-genisis. At Edinburgh Charles found the medical lectures 'intolerably dull'.

So it came about that his father realized that he was not going to make a doctor and decided that he should become a minister instead, sending him in 1828 to Christ's College, Cambridge, to read for a pass degree in Divinity. Whilst, as he tells us, he spent much of his time at Cambridge riding, shooting, and collecting beetles, he became a friend of J. S. Henslow, Professor of Botany, who introduced him to Adam Sedgwick, Professor of Geology. It was their influence, it will be remembered, that largely removed his parents' objections to his going as naturalist on the *Beagle*.

In the previous chapter I have emphasized how important was the reading of Charles Lyell's *Principles of Geology* during the voyage, and then how he came to think of the possibility of evolution by seeing the excavation of the fossil skeletons of extinct mammals and their similarity to living forms, by seeing the differences in the birds and reptiles on the various islands of the Galapagos group and also his being fascinated by the adaptions of insects to their environment in the Brazilian forests.

On his return from the *Beagle* he began the famous notebook 'for the collection of facts which bore in any way on the variation in animals and plants under domestication and in nature'. He had been struck by man's powers of developing various characters in domestic animals by selective breeding. Could there not be some similar principle operating in nature, he thought? In 1838 when reading Malthus[7] on population, he realized how selection in nature could

---

[7] Malthus (1766–1834), mathematician, social economist and parson, first published his *Essay on the Principle of Population* anonymously in 1798 and then a much larger and altered edition, using his name, in 1803. He showed that life tended to increase in a geometrical progression and that, unless there were severe checks on the population, man would soon out-strip his food supply; such checks being unwholesome occupations, severe labour, extreme poverty, diseases, war, famines, etc.

be brought about[8]. We read in his autobiography[9] as follows:

> In October 1838, that is, fifteen months after I had begun my systematic enquiry, I happened to read for amusement Malthus on *Population* and, being well prepared to appreciate the struggle for existence which everywhere goes on from long-continued observation of the habits of animals and plants, it at once struck me that under these circumstances favourable variations would tend to be preserved, and unfavourable ones to be destroyed. The result of this would be the formation of new species. Here, then, I had at last got a theory by which to work; but I was so anxious to avoid prejudice, that I determined not for some time to write even the briefest sketch of it. In June 1842 I first allowed myself the satisfaction of writing a very brief abstract of my theory in pencil in 35 pages; and this was enlarged during the summer of 1844 into one of 230 pages, which I had fairly copied out and still possess.

He sent a copy of this last essay to Lyell who begged him to publish it and warned him that if he delayed much longer he would surely be forestalled by someone; Darwin, however, would go on collecting more and more facts to support his theory before committing himself and ten more years went by. He also sent a copy of his essay to his friend Sir Joseph Hooker, the botanist who had just returned from accompanying the famous *Erebus* and *Terror* expedition to the Antarctic. Darwin's greatness was twofold: firstly in working out his theory of natural selection and secondly his patient marshalling of as much material as he could collect before going into print.

[8] Sir Gavin de Beer has recently shown (in his book, *Charles Darwin*, 1963) that the idea actually came to Darwin a little earlier, but it was Malthus who made him realize the force it could have, as is clearly shown in the quotation I give from his autobiography.

[9] *The Autobiography of Charles Darwin*, edited by N. Barlow, Collins, 1958, p. 120.

Whilst most readers will be familiar with the essence of his theory of selection, it may be well for me to give a brief summary of it at this point. He called it *natural* selection because he had been so struck by man's power of selecting and breeding from those variations of domestic animals which would be of greater value to him, such as breeds of sheep having thicker coats of wool, hens with higher egg yield and so on. He felt that there must be some factor in nature which made a similar kind of selection to lead eventually to new species of animals – to give us in fact (as he then thought) the origin of species. As we have just seen Malthus gave him the clue and in contrast to man's selection he called it natural selection. In outline we may describe the theory in the following terms: animals and plants tend to vary in all sorts of ways and some of these variations are inherited from one generation to another. They reproduce at such a rate that there is intensive competition for available supplies of food – only a very small proportion can survive to maturity. Some varieties will be more successful in the struggle for life than others; they will tend to survive – to be, as Darwin said, selected by nature – and so to contribute more to posterity. The less efficient strains will tend to be eliminated and will consequently appear less often in the ancestry of future generations.

Darwin went on steadily collecting his facts as if he had all the time in the world before him, but in 1855 Wallace begins to come into the story. Before passing to him, however, I feel I should reveal what to me was a very unexpected episode in the Darwin story when first I heard of it and one which I believe is not well known to the general public and indeed perhaps only familiar to a limited number of biologists. It concerns the vital part which Darwin's visit to the Galapagos Islands played in the formation of his views. Somehow one had imagined that he was at once struck by the differences between the reptiles and birds of the various islands and that this immediately set him thinking; this was not so at all. Apparently he did not notice the differences until a chance remark from the Vice-Governor of the islands drew his attention to the differences in the giant tortoises; he then noticed that the mocking birds from each island varied somewhat in form. The differences between the many kinds of finches, which turned out to be so very important, were not noticed by Darwin until the collections he had made were examined by the specialist, J. Gould, who pointed them out after his return to England. Let me allow the late James Ritchie, Regius Professor of Natural History in the University of Edinburgh, tell the story by quoting from his paper in the *University of Edinburgh Journal*, 1943, pp. 97–105.

He begins by saying 'Often it seems as if a great discovery hung upon a thread, as if the merest accident . . . had turned a human mind along a line of thought . . . Almost by such a slender tie are the insignificant but now memorable islands of Galapagos linked with the origin of the theory of evolution.' Now let me give his account of Darwin's visit:

It was almost an accident that led to the forging of the chain which bound Galapagos to evolution. The discrimination of closely related forms of animal life demands great knowledge of minute characteristics as well as acute observation, and Darwin, thrown into an unfamiliar fauna, failed to notice that the different islands of the group possessed many distinctive varieties of their own. So he began by lumping together the collections he made from different islands, regarding the whole as a single collecting unit. It was a natural thing to do, but it was an error which, persisted in, would have destroyed the evidence of what he himself afterwards described as 'by far the most remarkable feature in the natural history of this archipelago'.

Then he met an Englishman, Mr Lawson, the Vice-Governor of the islands, charged with the care of a newly-founded colony of two or three hundred souls, who pointed out to him that the giant tortoises from the different islands were themselves different, and that, shown a tortoise, he could tell without hesitation from which island it had been brought. Ten years later, in his *Journal of the Voyage*, Darwin thus recorded his own reaction to this remarkable observation: 'I did not for some time pay sufficient attention to this statement, and I had already partially mingled together the collections from two of the islands. I never dreamed that islands, about fifty or sixty miles apart, and most of them in sight of each other, formed of precisely the same rocks, placed under a quite similar climate, rising to a nearly equal height, would have been differently tenanted. . . . It is the fate of most voyagers, no sooner to discover what is most interesting in any locality, than they are hurried from it; but I ought, perhaps, to be thankful that I obtained sufficient materials to establish this most remarkable fact in the distribution of organic beings' (*Journal*, chap. xvii).

Nevertheless, this most remarkable fact, the focussing point of the evolutionary interest of the islands, as we now see, was slow in gaining appreciation. When Gould first described the birds which Darwin discovered there, he recorded them all as simply from Galapagos, although the island birds form one of the most significant series in the evolutionary story. And Darwin, when he wrote the *Journal of the Voyage*, still spoke of 'the amount of creative force, if such an expression may be used, displayed on these small, barren and rocky islands'.

So, looking back, we commend the shrewd observation of Mr Lawson; that was a thread upon which Darwin's later thoughts were strung. It is an odd reflection upon the growth of an idea which transformed the thinking of the world, that it should have rested upon the casual information of the Vice-Governor of the Galapagos Islands, in the absence of which the collections from the different islands would have been commingled and the all important evidence lost.

The late Dr David Lack in his splendid book *Darwin's Finches* (Cambridge University Press, 1947) fully confirms and adds to this account as follows:

Darwin first questioned the mutability of species when actually in the Galapagos, through finding different forms of the mocking-bird and tortoise on different islands[10]. The finches, with several species on each island, are more complex, and their influence was apparently retrospective. Thus, in Darwin's private diary of the voyage, the finches are not mentioned,[11] and even in the first published edition of the *Journal*, in 1839, they receive only brief notice, without particular comment. However, this paragraph was considerably amplified in the second edition of 1845: 'The remaining land-birds form a most singular group of finches, related to each other in the structure of their beaks, short tails, form of body and plumage. All these species are peculiar to this archipelago.' Darwin went on to describe 'the perfect gradation in the size of the beaks in the different species', and concluded: 'Seeing this gradation and diversity of structure in one small, intimately related group of birds, one might really fancy that from an original paucity of birds in this archipelago, one species had been taken and modified for different ends.' This last phrase is the most significant in the whole book, and is Darwin's first public pronouncement on a subject the elaboration and generalization of which was to occupy the next fifteen years of his life.

I shall be returning to the differences between the species of Darwin's Galapagos finches when I come to consider what

[10] N. Barlow, *Nature*, Vol. 136, p. 391, 1935.
[11] N. Barlow, *Charles Darwin's Diary of the Voyage of HMS Beagle*, pp. xiii, 333–43, 1933.

I call 'behavioural selection' in Chapter 7 (p. 145). At some point, and this may be as good a place as any, I want to stress the greatness of Darwin as a naturalist quite apart from his work on the theory of evolution; Darwin I believe is the greatest naturalist who has ever lived. I have already referred (p. 29) to his monumental monograph on the barnacles, but then, in a remarkable series of volumes, each a classic, he described his observational and experimental studies in the natural history of both plants and animals. A century ago almost every educated person would have known something of the scope of his prodigious work, but today, I fear, it it less familiar to the general public; to give an idea of this range let met first quote the titles of his books (other than on evolution) – *The Fertilization of Orchids* (1862), *The Expression of the Emotions in Man and Animals* (1873), *The Formation of Vegetable Mould through the action of Worms* (1881), *Insectivorous Plants* (1875), *Climbing Plants* (1875), *The Effects of Cross and Self Fertilization in the Vegetable Kingdom* (1876), *Different Forms of Flowers in Plants of the same Species* (1877), *The Power of Movement in Plants* (1880).

Let me now take up the story again where Wallace enters it. Alfred Russel Wallace was born in 1823 at Usk in Monmouthshire and on leaving school he worked as a land surveyor and architect. At the age of about seventeen he became interested in natural history and began to make a herbarium of wild flowers, and then in 1844 he became an English master at the Collegiate School at Leicester where he met the naturalist H. W. Bates who set him off collecting beetles. Wallace never went to a university, nor did Darwin have any formal instruction in biology except the beginnings of the medical course he abandoned at Edinburgh; Darwin, as I have reminded you, also began by collecting beetles at Cambridge as he worked for his pass degree in theology. There seems to be a curious fascination about beetles. Wallace's passion for natural history grew and in 1848 he and Bates went off on an expedition to the Amazon; he had decided to make his career that of collecting zoological and botanical specimens for museums and private collections. In 1850 he set out to return to England with a large collection but disaster struck when his ship caught fire; he escaped with his life but his whole collection was lost. Most men would have been discouraged by an arduous two years' work, assembling the marvellous riches of the tropical forests, all being reduced to ashes; not so with Wallace, however, for in 1854 he set out again on a similar mission, but this time to the Malay Archipelago.

I must now go a little more slowly for I am anxious, in this brief history of thought leading up to our present views, to give Wallace what I feel to be a rather fairer proportion of the credit for the history of selection than has usually been allotted him outside strictly biological circles. Whilst collecting in the forest of Sarawak, in 1855, he had a paper published in the *Annals and Magazine of Natural History* entitled 'On the Law which has regulated the Introduction of New Species'; his main conclusions were that 'every species has come into existence coincident both in space and time with a pre-existing closely allied species.' The high merits of this paper were discussed by the late Professor C. P. A. Pantin who writes: 'The importance of this essay is twofold. It is perhaps the most important "pre-Darwinian" essay on the origin of species apart from the works of Lamarck. Further, taken together with his 1858 essay it shows that Wallace did not merely contribute the notion of natural selection but had in effect a complete skeleton for a work on the origin of species such as Darwin possessed at the time of his 1842 essay.'[12] It attracted much attention; and Darwin entered into friendly correspondence with Wallace telling him that for a long time he had been collecting facts bearing on the question of the origin of species, but he gave no hint whatever of his theory of natural selection. He had kept it a secret from all but three: first Lyell, then Hooker and lastly a rough sketch sent to Asa Gray in 1857.

[12] *Proceedings of the Linnean Society of London*, vol. 171, p. 139, 1960.

In the spring of 1858, Wallace lay sick of fever at Ternate in the Island of Celebes and his thoughts wandered to the species problem. He then remembered Malthus, whose book he had read twelve years before, and I will continue the story with an extract from his *My Life* (1908):

> Then I thought of the enormously rapid multiplication of animals, causing these checks to be much more effective in them than in the case of man; and while pondering vaguely on this fact there suddenly flashed upon me the *idea* of the survival of the fittest – that the individuals removed by these checks must be on the whole inferior to those that survived. In the two hours that elapsed before my ague fit was over, I had thought out almost the whole of the theory; and the same evening I sketched the draft of my paper, and in the two succeeding evenings wrote it out in full, and sent it by the next post to Mr Darwin.

The title he gave to his manuscript paper was 'On the tendency of variations to depart indefinitely from the original type'.

The paper arrived at a very bad time for Darwin. He was ill himself and very depressed; an infant son had died the day before of scarlet fever and a little daughter was dangerously ill with diphtheria. On his breakfast plate lay the letter from Wallace enclosing the paper and asking him to send it on to Lyell. Darwin was flabbergasted and wrote hurriedly to Lyell:

> . . . your words have come true with a vengeance – that I should be forestalled . . . I never saw a more striking coincidence; if Wallace had my MS. sketch written out in 1842, he could not have made a better short abstract! Even his terms now stand as heads of my chapters. Please return me the MS. which he does not say he wishes me to publish, but I shall of course at once write and offer to send it to any journal. So all my originality,

whatever it may amount to, will be smashed, although my book, if it will ever have any value, will not be deteriorated; as all the labour consists in the application of the theory.

In a second letter to Lyell (25 June) he says:

But as I had not intended to publish my sketch, can I do so honourably, because Wallace has sent me an outline of his doctrine? I would far rather burn my whole book than that he or any other man should think that I had behaved in a paltry spirit. Do you think his having sent me this sketch ties my hands? . . .

and next day, he wrote to Lyell yet again:

Forgive me for adding a P.S. . . . First impressions are generally right, and I at first thought it would be dishonourable in me now to publish.

Darwin would have held back his own work if he had not been persuaded to do otherwise by Hooker and Lyell who both knew of his essay written years before Wallace's. He left the matter in their hands and the two papers, Darwin's and Wallace's, were read together at the meeting of the Linnean Society on 1 July 1858.

How did this historic event strike the contemporary scientific world? Was their exciting new conception loudly acclaimed? Not a bit of it. It fell completely flat. So complete was the lack of appreciation and with such pomposity was it expressed that, on looking back, it can only be described, I think, as comic. It is almost as if some cruel demon had inspired the president of the Society (none other than Thomas Bell the great crustacean expert) to go out of his way to make so crass an error of judgement. In his address, on 24 May 1859, reviewing the past year of the Society's proceedings, he said:

This year . . . has not indeed been marked by any of those striking discoveries which at once revolutionize, so to speak, the department of science on which they bear; it is only at remote intervals that we can reasonably expect any sudden and brilliant innovation which shall produce a marked and permanent impress on the character of any branch of knowledge or confer a lasting and important service on mankind. A Bacon or a Newton, an Oersted or a Wheatstone, a Davy or a Daguerre, is an occasional phenomenon, whose existence and career seem to be especially appointed by Providence for the purpose of effecting some great important change in the conditions or the pursuits of men.[13]

Darwin published his *Origin of Species* in November of the following year, 1859. It was his marshalling of such an enormous body of facts in support, from so many different fields, together with his giving the first reasonable and simple theory of its working, that convinced the thinking world of the reality of evolution. Even the great T. H. Huxley was not fully convinced in the summer of '59[14] (a year after Darwin's and Wallace's papers) but upon reading the *Origin* he was won over as we see from his brilliant three and a half column review of the book in *The Times* of 26 December of that year. In the following summer, at the British Association meeting in Oxford, came Huxley's debate with Bishop Wilberforce which had been thought to have rocked the intellectual world, but did it?; I return to it at the end of the chapter.

For all the patient labour in preparing the case and for its masterly presentation Darwin must get the greater credit, but for brilliance of insight Wallace, I believe, should get more acknowledgement than he has received. Some years later, when Darwin was working on his theory of sexual

[13] *Proceedings of the Linnean Society of London*, 1858–9, p. viii.
[14] See Pantin, *Proc. Linn. Soc. London*, 1959, p. 222.

selection and trying to explain all bright colouring of animals by this means, he came to consider the many gaily adorned caterpillars and then, of course, realized that at this stage they had no sex life at all! He wrote in his perplexity to Wallace, and by return of post came the theory of warning coloration which in all essentials is just as it is accepted today; in fact as now proved correct by experiment. I think it worth recording more fully.

We see in *The Life and Letters of Charles Darwin* (vol. III, pp. 93–4) that he wrote to Wallace on 23 February 1867 saying, 'On Monday evening I called on Bates, and put a difficulty before him, which he could not answer and, as on some former similar occasion, his first suggestion was, "You had better ask Wallace." My difficulty is, why are caterpillars sometimes so beautifully and artistically coloured? . . .'

On 26 February Darwin had obviously had Wallace's reply for he writes, 'My dear Wallace, Bates was quite right; you are the man to apply to in a difficulty. I never heard anything more ingenious than your suggestion . . .'

When we think of the theory of natural selection we must never forget the name of Alfred Russel Wallace. What a wonderful pair of men they were: Darwin who, after twenty years' hard work on his theory, was prepared to withdraw completely to let Wallace have the priority; and Wallace, who, if he had had a different character, might so easily have demanded his right to have his work published first, used as the title of his most important book on evolution, just one word: *Darwinism*!

How remarkably similar their two independent accounts of the theory were can only be appreciated by carefully comparing the two papers. Osborn in his *From the Greeks to Darwin* has done this by showing side by side, in summary form, the relevant passages from each version; I reproduce this as follows:

DARWIN	WALLACE
There is in Nature a struggle for existence as shown by Malthus and De Candolle. Rapid multiplication, if unchecked, even in slow breeding animals like the elephant . . .	The life of wild animals is a struggle for existence . . . in which the weakest and least perfect must always succumb. Even the least prolific animals increase rapidly if unchecked.
Great changes in the environment occur.	A change in the environment may occur.
It has been shown in a former part of this work that such changes of external conditions would, from their acting upon the reproductive system, probably cause the organization . . . to become plastic.	(No cause of variation assigned)
	Varieties do frequently occur spontaneously.
Can it be doubted . . . any innate variation in structure, habits, or instincts, adapting the individual better to the new conditions, would tell upon its vigour and health. In the struggle it would have a better chance of surviving; and those of the offspring who inherited the variation, be it ever so slight, would also have a better chance.	All variations from the typical form have some definite effect, however slight, on the habits and capacities of the individuals. Abundance or rarity of a species is dependent on its more or less perfect adaptation. If any species should produce a variety having slightly increased powers of preserving existence, that variety must inevitably in time acquire a superiority in numbers.

As Osborn pointed out, remarkable as the parallelism is, it is not complete. Darwin dwells upon variations in single characters as taken hold of by selection whereas Wallace is more concerned with *full formed varieties* as being favourably or unfavourably adapted.

Looking back, fifty years after the joint publication of

their two papers, Wallace, at the age of 85, makes a contribution to the Darwin–Wallace jubilee celebration volume published by the Linnean Society and modestly compares their two qualities. 'I was then, as often since,' he said, 'the "young man" in a hurry; he [Darwin] the painstaking and patient student, seeking ever the full demonstration of the truth he had discovered, rather than to achieve immediate personal fame.' And later in the same article he referred to their relative share of the credit for the initiation of the principle of natural selection and suggests as a fair proportion a ratio of 'twenty years to one week', those being the periods each had devoted to it. He also showed (in the same volume) how much he too was indebted to Lyell:

> Along with Malthus I had read, and been even more deeply impressed by, Sir Charles Lyell's immortal *Principles of Geology*; which had taught me that the inorganic world – the whole surface of the earth, its seas and lands, its mountains and valleys, its rivers and lakes, and every detail of its climatic conditions – were and always had been in a continual state of slow modification. Hence it became obvious that the forms of life must have become continually adjusted to these changed conditions in order to survive.

Some critics at once doubted whether there really was the great destruction of life implied by natural selection. They doubted whether selection could normally be so severe as to bring about the changes postulated, changes similar to those brought about by man by his continual selective breeding. Wallace, who like Darwin had been so much influenced by Malthus, well answered such critics[15] with the following simple example. A bird like a sparrow usually lays six eggs in a clutch and usually has two or more broods in a year; and in captivity, they will live for over fifteen years. Let us be conservative, said Wallace, and suppose that they only live

[15] In *Darwinism*, p. 25.

ten years and only produce ten young a year. If all these young grew up to lead a natural breeding life and if on an average half of them are females, a simple little sum will show that in ten years' time for every pair of sparrows today, there will be over 24 million as shown in table II. Yet we know that the sparrows are not usually increasing. This, of course, does not mean that for every two sparrows over 24 million will die in the next ten years, because, out of each ten offspring per year, to keep the balance right, there will be a loss, on an average, of eight or nine. Over thousands of years this gives plenty of scope for selection; those variations that are the more efficiently adapted for their life will, more often than not, tend to survive. Compared with many other animals a bird like a sparrow has relatively few offspring; there are many insects that lay a thousand eggs and some whose hatching grubs become mature adults within a fortnight. The codfish lays a million eggs and the halibut five million! We can have no doubt that the competition for food is great.

In his first edition of the *Origin* Darwin relied almost entirely on natural selection to bring about the evolutionary change. In his sixth edition of 1872, however, he had come to

TABLE II

Original parent birds	2
1st generation	10
2nd generation	50
3rd generation	250
4th generation	1,250
5th generation	6,250
6th generation	31,250
7th generation	156,250
8th generation	781,250
9th generation	3,906,250
10th generation	19,531,250
Total (if all remained alive)	24,414,062

admit the importance of the use and disuse effect (which was Lamarck's theory, although he does not acknowledge it) and on p. 395 summarizes his views thus:

> This [evolution] has been effected chiefly through the natural selection of numerous successive, slight, favourable variations, aided in an important manner by the inherited effects of use and disuse of parts; and in an unimportant manner, that is in relation to adaptive structures, whether past or present, by the direct action of external conditions [this was Buffon's theory], and by variations which seem to us in our ignorance to arise quite spontaneously.

It is certainly interesting to note this change when we remember that in 1844 he wrote to Hooker saying 'Heaven defend me from Lamarck's nonsense' and in other letters of the same period he refers to Lamarck's work as 'veritable rubbish' and 'an absurd though clever book'. This weakening of his position in regard to natural selection was due to a criticism published in 1867. Not much general notice of this objection, however, was taken until much later, and for this reason I postpone an account of it (p. 87); nevertheless it affected Darwin deeply. Wallace was clearly shocked at Darwin's retreat. I have recorded how Wallace had modestly and generously called his most important work on evolution by the simple title *Darwinism*; I should also say that I think there was, in addition, just a touch of irony in it, for in his preface to this book he shows that he was now more Darwinian than Darwin:

> Although I maintain [he writes] and even enforce my differences from some of Darwin's views, my whole work tends forcibly to illustrate the overwhelming importance of natural selection over all other agencies in the production of new species. I thus take up Darwin's earlier position, from which he somewhat receded in the later editions of his works, on account of criticism

69

and objections which I have endeavoured to show are unsound. Even in rejecting that phase of sexual selection depending on female choice, I insist on the greater efficacy of natural selection. This is pre-eminently the Darwinian doctrine, and I therefore claim for my book the position of being the advocate of pure Darwinism.

I have already (p. 56) given a somewhat formal statement of the essence of Darwin and Wallace's theory of natural selection. I will now give some very simple examples of its working. I will show how, over long periods of time, the most remarkable adaptations can be produced entirely as the result of what appear to be random inherited variations being acted upon by the selective powers of an entirely physical environment. I want to emphasize how important it is that the general public should realize how a great deal of evolution, possibly well over 95 per cent taking all the lower organisms into account, is to be explained in terms of selection by external events, both physical and animate. It is a fact that a great deal of the process of evolution can be reduced to physical and chemical terms; if we don't realize this our whole outlook on life will be warped. Let me say at once, as I believe the later parts of the book will show, that this reductionism will *not* explain the more important part of life; we must first, however, appreciate how amazingly *creative* the entirely material process may be – so much so that as I think we shall see, we might be tempted to use the word 'inventive' which of course would be wrong.

I take as my examples the adaptations of seeds for aerial distribution. Let me trace step by step the changes that must have taken place in their production. First imagine a seed falling straight to the ground and then imagine a chance variation occurring which provides it with some hair-like processes so that, if there is even a slight breeze, it will be carried a little way to right or left according to the direction of the wind; if the variations are of a hereditary kind, then over a number of generations such variations may tend to survive better than the progeny of those with smooth surfaces because they will fall on a variety of different types of ground, some of which may be more favourable than others. Now over long periods of time the seeds with a greater production of hair-like processes will be characteristic of the species. If, by chance, variations should appear giving more hairs on one end of the seed than the other end, such seeds will tend to hang below their crown of hairs like a parachute and so float better in the air and get carried further and further; now after millions of years of chance, inherited variation, the form of the parachute will continually be improved to give us the beautiful buoyant seeds of the dandelion or thistle which may be carried for miles and miles over the countryside on summer days with only the gentlest breezes.

By a similar gradual process the gyrating seeds of the sycamore have been gradually evolved from seeds which first by chance were provided with a little flange which set them spinning in the wind when they were released; again, after long periods of time, they became more and more like an auto-gyro flying almost horizontally for quite a distance in a good wind. Still more wonderful are the gliding seeds of some tropical conifers; I cannot resist a little anecdote. My best friend at school was Alan Gardiner, the son of the famous Cambridge botanist, Walter Gardiner who was a Fellow of Clare. Once, when I stayed with them in the holidays, his father took us boys up on the roof of the college and broke open one of the cones; as the seeds came out, each was wrapped in what looked like a folded parchment which at once sprang open, like the spreading of the wings of a butterfly, to produce in a flash a paper glider, beautifully shaped with the seed in the middle of its front edge. Launched in the air each one glided in a gradually descending path, sometimes rising slightly to swoop down again; some went for nearly a hundred yards and one I remember actually crossed the Cam. These designs show just how creative natural selection can be; they might have come straight out of Leonardo's sketch books.

I have made this little digression for a purpose: to illustrate the power of selection and I hope show the general reader that the idea so often given by some biologists that it is the random genetic variations that are governing the course of evolution is quite wrong. These random genetic changes in any population of animals or plants are providing the almost infinite range of variation upon which selection can act. It is selection which guides the process and *not* the random mutations; we should note too that selection itself is far from random. Given time – and there is plenty of time – selection, of many different kinds as we shall later see, can produce all the adaptational wonders of the living world.

Selection is certainly the key to the physical side of evolution. Because so many of those truly remarkable adaptive creations can be shown to be produced by the selective powers of either the physical environment or of the action of other organisms – predators or competitors – so many biologists seem to feel that there is surely no need to look further; they become blind to other possibilities. The kind of selection which I believe has been almost entirely overlooked is one to which I have given the name of 'behavioural selection'. It is this that I believe may be so important in relating evolution theory to the spiritual side of man, as I think we shall agree as the book develops in its later stages.

I must now say a little more about the brilliant insight of Alfred Russel Wallace; this time in relation to the evolution of man. He came to realize the fundamental change that had taken place in the very nature of the evolutionary process long before others had grasped its full signficance. He put forward his ideas in 1864 in a paper in the *Anthropological Review* (vol. 2, pp. clviii–clxx), a journal which most unfortunately soon ceased to exist. I shall quote from it at some length because it is only to be found in a limited number of libraries and has been largely forgotten. We should remember that it was published only five years after Darwin's *Origin of Species* and seven years *before* Darwin's *The Descent of Man*; it bore the title 'The Origin of Human Races and the

Antiquity of Man Deduced from the Theory of Natural Selection'.

Thus man, [he wrote] by the mere capacity of clothing himself, and making weapons and tools, has taken away from nature that power of changing the external form and structure which she exercises over all other animals. As the competing races by which they are surrounded, the climate, the vegetation, or the animals which serve them for food, are slowly changing, they must undergo a corresponding change in their structure, habits, and constitution, to keep them in harmony with the new conditions – to enable them to live and maintain their numbers. But man does this by means of his intellect alone; which enables him with an unchanged body still to keep in harmony with the changing universe.

From the time, therefore, when the social and sympathetic feelings came into active operation, and the intellectual and moral faculties became fairly developed, man would cease to be influenced by 'natural selection' in his physical form and structure; as an animal he would remain almost stationary; the changes of the surrounding universe would cease to have upon him that powerful modifying effect which it exercises over other parts of the organic world. But from the moment that his body became stationary, his mind would become subject to those very influences from which his body had escaped; every slight variation in his mental and moral nature which should enable him better to guard against adverse circumstances, and combine for mutual comfort and protection, would be preserved and accumulated; the better and higher specimens of our race would therefore increase and spread, the lower and more brutal would give way and successively die out, and that rapid advancement of mental organization would occur, which has raised the very lowest races of man so far above the brutes . . .

If the views I have here endeavoured to sustain have any foundation, they give us a new argument for placing man apart as not only the head and culminating point of the grand series of organic nature, but as in some degree a new and distinct order of being. From those infinitely remote ages, when the first rudiments of organic life appeared upon the earth, every plant and every animal has been subject to one great law of physical change. As the earth has gone through its grand cycles of geological, climatal and organic progress, every form of life has been subject to its irresistible action, and has been continually but imperceptibly moulded into such new shapes as would preserve their harmony with the ever-changing universe. No living thing could escape this law of its being; none could remain unchanged and live, amid the universal change around it.

At length, however, there came into existence a being in whom that subtle force we term *mind* became of greater importance than his mere bodily structure. Though with a naked and unprotected body, *this* gave him clothing against the varying inclemencies of the seasons. Though unable to compete with the deer in swiftness, or with the wild bull in strength, *this* gave him weapons with which to capture or overcome both. Though less capable than most other animals of living on the herbs and the fruits that unaided nature supplies, this wonderful faculty taught him to govern and direct nature to his own benefit, and make her produce food for him when and where he pleased. From the moment when the first skin was used as a covering, when the first rude spear was formed to assist in the chase, the first seed sown or shoot planted, a grand revolution was effected in nature, a revolution which in all the previous ages of the earth's history had had no parallel, for a being had arisen who was no longer necessarily subject to change with the changing universe – a being who

74

was in some degree superior to nature, inasmuch as he knew how to control and regulate her action and could keep himself in harmony with her, not by a change in body, but by an advance of mind.

Here, then, we see the true grandeur and dignity of man. On this view of his special attributes, we may admit that even those who claim for him a position as an order, a class, or a sub-kingdom by himself, have some reason on their side. He is, indeed, a being apart, since he is not influenced by the great laws which irresistibly modify all other organic beings. Nay more; this victory which he has gained for himself gives him a directing influence over other existences. Man has not only escaped 'natural selection' himself, but he actually is able to take away some of that power from nature which, before his appearance, she universally exercised. We can anticipate the time when the earth will produce only cultivated plants and domestic animals; when man's selection shall have supplanted 'natural selection'; and when the ocean will be the only domain in which that power can be exerted, which for countless cycles of ages ruled supreme over all the earth.

Darwin was delighted with the paper and wrote on 22 May 1864 to Hooker:

I have now read Wallace's paper on Man, and think it *most* striking and original and forcible. I wish he had written Lyell's chapters on Man . . . I am not sure that I fully agree with his views about Man, but there is no doubt, in my opinion, on the remarkable genius shown by the paper. I agree, however, to the main new leading idea.

and on 28 May he wrote to Wallace:

. . . But now for your Man paper, about which I should like to write more than I can. The great leading idea is quite new to me – viz. that during late ages the mind will have been modified more than the body; yet I had got as far as to see with you that the struggle between the races of man depended entirely on intellectual and moral qualities. The latter part of the paper I can designate only as grand and most eloquently done . . . I am not sure that I go with you on all minor points . . .

Wallace replied at length to Darwin's criticisms and clarified his views regarding the lesser points raised.

In introducing this long quotation from Wallace's paper I said that he had here realized long before any other biologists had done so, that with the coming of man a fundamental change had taken place in the very nature of the evolutionary process. Nearly a hundred years were to pass before various leaders in the field of evolutionary studies came to the same conclusion. The views of four of these later writers, Sir Julian Huxley, Sir Peter Medawar, C. H. Waddington and Richard Dawkins, will be discussed later in the book (pp. 168–77).

Concerning the nature of man, Wallace towards the end of his life gave a very clear summing up of the difference between his views and those of Darwin; this comes in the second volume of his autobiography *My Life*, p. 17, 1905, where he writes as follows:

On this great problem the belief and teaching of Darwin was that man's whole nature – physical, mental, intellectual, and moral – was developed from the lower animals by the means of the same laws of variation and survival; and as a consequence of this belief, that there was no difference in *kind* between man's nature and animal nature, but only one of degree. My view, on the other hand, was, and is, that there is a difference in kind, intellectually and morally, between man and other animals; and that while his body was undoubtedly developed by the continuous modification of some ancestral animal form, some different agency, analagous to that which first produced organic *life*, and then originated *consciousness*, came into play in order to develop the higher intellectual and spiritual nature of man.

It is indeed with this agency which first produced organic *life* and originated *consciousness* and then led to the *spiritual nature of man* that this book is really all about.

Presently in Chapter 5 I shall be going on to the subsequent developments leading up to the neo-Darwinian position of today; I will now end this one by giving some new facts about that famous debate which took place at the British Association meeting at Oxford in 1860 when T. H. Huxley and Bishop Wilberforce clashed in a discussion of Darwin's *The Origin of Species*. It has often been regarded as marking the point in history when Darwinism won so brilliant a victory that from that day onwards the greater part of the intellectual world accepted evolution as a reality. What do we actually know for certain about that event? Those who read *The Historical Journal* will know something of the answer; and I feel sure they will have been as surprised as I was when I read it. In the issue of 2 February 1979, pp. 315–30, my friend, the Oxford philosopher, John R. Lucas, contributed a paper entitled 'Wilberforce and Huxley: a legendary encounter', in which he gives us the results of his research into records. He has kindly allowed me to give some quotations; before doing so, however, I must call attention to another quite independent and slightly later paper on the same subject, drawing on some fresh material but giving good support to Lucas's thesis. It is by Dr Sheridan Gilley of the Department of Theology of the University of Durham and is in *Religious and Humanism Studies in Church History*, Vol. 17, pp. 325–40 (Blackwell, Oxford, 1981). Is it not remarkable that after some 120 years since the debate, two scholars, quite independently, should at the same time be going back to look at the evidence? Almost reminiscent of Darwin and Wallace. Now let me proceed to the quotations from Lucas.

The legend is well given [he says] in the October 1898 issue of *Macmillan's Magazine*, in an article entitled 'A Grandmother's tales'.[16] In the course of this . . . the writer relates

I was happy enough to be present on the memorable occasion at Oxford when Mr Huxley bearded Bishop Wilberforce. There were so many of us that were eager to hear that we had to adjourn to the great library of the Museum. I can still hear the American accents of Dr Draper's opening address, when he asked 'Air we a fortuitous concourse of atoms?' and his discourse I seem to remember as somewhat dry. Then the Bishop rose, and in a light, scoffing tone, florid and fluent, he assured us there was nothing in the idea of evolution; rock-pigeons were what rock-pigeons had always been. Then, turning to his antagonist with a smiling insolence, he begged to know, was it through his grandfather or his grandmother that he claimed his descent from a monkey? On this Mr Huxley slowly and deliberately arose. A slight, tall figure, stern and pale, very quiet and very grave, he stood before us, and spoke those tremendous words – words which no one seems sure of now, nor I think, could remember just after they were spoken, for their meaning took away our breath, though it left us in no doubt as to what it was. He was not ashamed to have a monkey for his ancestor; but he would be ashamed to be connected with a man who used great gifts to obscure the truth. No one doubted his meaning and the effect was tremendous. One lady fainted and had to be carried out: I, for one, jumped out of my seat . . .

[16] By Mrs Isabella Sidgwick, *Macmillan's Magazine*, LXXVIII, no, 468, October 1898, 'A Grandmother's tales', 433–4. I owe the identification to Mr Christopher Chessun of University College, Oxford.

Sir Joseph Hooker supplied substantially similar accounts for the official biographies of Darwin[17] and Huxley.[18] He tells us:

> The famous Oxford Meeting of 1860 was of no small importance in Huxley's career. It was not merely that he helped to save a great cause from being stifled under misrepresentation and ridicule – that he helped to extort for it a fair hearing; it was now that he first made himself known in popular estimation as a dangerous adversary in debate – a personal force in the world of science which could not be neglected. From this moment he entered the front fighting line in the most exposed quarter of the field.[19]

This last quotation from Hooker of what he wrote so much later is in extraordinary contrast to what he wrote to Darwin on the very day following the debate, as we shall see in a moment after Lucas has discussed the reports of journalists who were actually present at the debate. He (Lucas) continues his account thus:

> Besides a number of letters to and from people in the Darwinian camp,[20] we have a journalist's report of the

[17] Francis Darwin, *Life and Letters of Charles Darwin* (3 vols., London, 1888), II, 320–3, hereafter cited as *Darwin*.
[18] Leonard Huxley, *Life and letters of Thomas Henry Huxley* (2 vols., London, 1900), I, 179–89, hereafter cited as *Huxley*.
[19] *Huxley*, I. 179.
[20] Hooker to Darwin on 2 July; reprinted in *Hooker*, I, 525–7. J. R. Green to W. Boyd Dawkins on 3 July; reprinted in L. Stephen (ed.), *Letters of J. R. Green* (London, 1901), pp. 42–5. Sir Charles Lyell to Sir Charles Bunbury on 4 July; reprinted in Mrs Lyell, *Life of Sir Charles Lyell* (London, 1881), II, 335; hereafter cited as *Lyell*. Huxley to Dyster on 9 September 1860, Huxley papers, Imperial College, London, 117 ff.; partly reprinted in Cyril Bibby, *Scientist Extraordinary*, *T. H. Huxley* (Oxford, 1972), p. 41. George Allman to Huxley, 9 July 1860, Huxley papers, 79. George Rolleston to Huxley, ? Dec. 1860, Huxley papers, 151 ff. I am much indebted to Professor Owen Chadwick for making copies of these letters available to me.

proceedings of the British Association in three issues of *The Athenaeum* and a briefer one in *Jackson's Oxford Journal*.[21] These accounts give a different picture. Neither of the journalists present reported those tremendous words or noted their tremendous effect. Although the opposed views of Wilberforce and Huxley on the nature of man were of great moment, and had been the topic of conversation throughout the week, and although the particular issue of the descent of man from the apes had been raised a couple of days earlier,[22] and although undoubtedly Wilberforce made some reference to apes, yet what he and Huxley actually said on that subject was not, in the opinion of a journalist actually reporting the debate, of sufficient interest to bear repetition.

Nor did it seem the next day sufficiently significant for Hooker to mention it in his letter to Darwin.[23] In Hooker's opinion – and the evidence of *The Athenaeum* and the opinion of Lyell[24] support this – it was he, not Huxley, who really answered Wilberforce. Hooker had become a Darwinian and announced his conversion at that meeting. He [Hooker] wrote unflatteringly of Wilberforce, and then continued: 'Huxley answered admirably and turned the tables, but he could not throw his voice over so large an assembly, nor command the audience; and he did not allude to Sam's weak points nor put the matter in a form or way that carried the audience. The battle waxed hot. Lady Brewster fainted, the excitement increased as others spoke; my blood boiled, I felt myself a dastard; now I saw my advantage; I swore to myself that I could smite that

---

[21] *The Athenaeum*, nos. 1705, 1706 and 1707, 30 June, 7 July and 14 July 1860. *Jackson's Oxford Journal*, Saturday 7 July, 1860, p. 2, col. 6.
[22] On Thursday, 28 June; see *The Athenaeum*, p. 26, col. i.
[23] *Hooker*, I, 525–7.
[24] *Lyell*, II, 335. See also The Rev. A. S. Farrar to Leonard Huxley, 12 July 1899, Huxley papers, 16.

Amalekite, Sam, hip and thigh if my heart jumped out of my mouth, and I handed my name up to the President (Henslow) as ready to throw down the gauntlet.'

Although later he gave all the credit to Huxley, at the time it seemed to him and to others that it was he rather than Huxley who fought most effectively for Darwin.

This paper is not only important in relation to the history of the concept of evolution. It provides us, I believe, with a valuable research into the extent and validity with which sayings may be repeated and held as gospel truth, or events recorded, some thirty or forty years after they were spoken, or had occurred.

4

The Real Origin of Species

If the last chapter was exceedingly long, the present one by being exceptionally short will help to restore the balance; I only want to make one point and a few paragraphs will suffice. The issue is better treated separately from the rest of the story; its purpose is to answer those critics who, in the recent discussions, would denigrate Darwin's position by saying that he was quite wrong to call his book *The Origin of Species* since he never really dealt with the actual process of species formation at all.

That is perfectly true, but it is unfair to blame him, for he honestly thought he was explaining the process, as we shall see; like everyone else of his time, he didn't understand the real nature of a species. Whilst I say 'like every one else', there *was* someone who gave a perfect definition of what species are and explained just how they originated; although published in 1825, it was then forgotten and apparently never discussed by the naturalists of Darwin's day. I will come to that explanation after I have shown how it was that Darwin and the other naturalists were mistaken. His book *The Origin* dealt primarily with the general principles of evolution. He did not recognize any real distinction between species and varieties on the one hand or between species and genera on the other; he regarded the development of such categories as one gradual general process with the distinction between them only a matter of classificatory convenience. Hardly anyone, until Ernst Mayr published his *Systematics and the Origin of Species* in 1942, really understood that the species was a unique unit, having quite a difference significance in the evolutionary system from that of any other category.

For a long time naturalists had accepted what had been called the practical species concept which Darwin held; he wrote in the *Origin of Species*: 'In determining whether a form should be ranked as a species or a variety, the opinion of naturalists having sound judgement and wide experience seems the only guide to follow.' We now realize that the species is something which is not just a matter of judgement but has a quite definite *objective reality*; it is a category which is not simply a convenience in classification – not just an arbitrary stage in the grouping of organisms in one series of differentiation of forms from small variations, through sub-species, species, genera, families and orders. It is now shown to be something quite different; it is, indeed, the *cardinal unit in the process of evolution*.

The crux of the matter is this. An interbreeding population of animals (or plants) may happen to become divided by a geographical barrier (or other means of isolation) into two quite separate groups, so that, with the passage of time, the members of one, by the action of selection under somewhat different conditions, may come to differ from those of the other; if eventually the two populations should come in contact with one another again, and if they should now be so different, either in structural or behavioural characters that they will no longer interbreed, then we shall have two new species in place of the former one. This is how the *real steps* in evolutionary change take place. It was, indeed, the separation of the slightly different forms of life on the Galapagos Islands which had subsequently, as we have seen, impressed Darwin so much and it was Wallace who made a special study of such isolation in his splendid book *Island Life*. It was not, however, until eighty years after Darwin's masterpiece was published that Mayr made us realize exactly how the origin of species did in fact take place. To illustrate this I reproduce in fig. 9 a simple diagram redrawn and somewhat re-arranged from his book; it will help to answer another of the criticisms

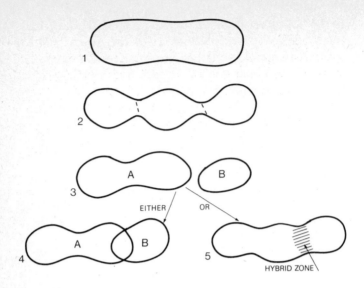

9. Stages in speciation. Redrawn from Ernst Mayr.

levelled against Darwin in the recent controversy. It explains why there are so few fossils to represent the transition from one species to another. The period of change from species A to species B is relatively short, perhaps only a few hundred years, compared with that of the existence of A and B as true species which may be many millions of years; the chances of there being fossil remains from the true species are so vastly greater than there being the chance fossil from the short transitional period.

If I were writing a text-book on evolution I should write pages on this process and reproduce some of the striking maps given by Mayr to demonstrate how such species formation has taken place in a number of different groups of birds; however, this is not such a treatise and what I have said will, I think, be sufficient to show how fundamental the species concept is. Isolation is the key.

It was Mayr, in his book, who told us how the conception

of the species had actually first been expressed, some ten years before Darwin ever went to the Galapagos, by the naturalist Leopold von Buch in a description of the fauna and flora of the Canary Islands published in 1825 (and then forgotten!):

> The individuals of a genus spread out over the continents, move to far-distant places, form varieties (on account of differences of the localities, of the food, and the soil), which owing to their segregation [geographical isolation] cannot interbreed with other varieties and thus be returned to the original main type. Finally these varieties become constant and turn into separate species. Later they may reach again the range of other varieties which have changed in a like manner, and the two will now no longer cross and thus they behave as 'two very different species'.

Again we may marvel how such a clear and simple statement on so important an issue can have lain unnoticed for so long. What else is lying neglected and forgotten, and what new things are round the corner? Quite a lot I am sure.

5

The Building
of Neo-Darwinism

We now tend to speak of neo-Darwinism to mark the distinction between our greater understanding of the nature of the evolutionary mechanism and what was known in Darwin's lifetime. The principle of natural selection, however, is just the same; what has changed is our greatly increased knowledge of the causes of the variations upon which it acts.

In the 1860s and '70s many people, whilst convinced of the realities of evolution through the writings of Darwin and Huxley, tended to prefer Lamarck's principle of the inheritance of the effects of use and disuse of parts of an animal's body (which I discussed on p. 50) rather than that of natural selection because they could not bring themselves to believe that the whole act of creation could be brought about by what seemed to be the ruthless, almost mechanical, selection of small chance variations.

Now in 1867 Professor Fleeming Jenkin, who was not a biologist at all, but Professor of Engineering in the University of Edinburgh, wrote a review of *The Origin of Species* in the *North British Review*; here he claimed to show that the theory of natural selection could not possibly work if the then generally accepted views on the nature of inheritance were true. These were the days before Mendel's work on heredity was known; his fundamental discoveries, whilst published in 1865 by the Natural History Society of Brünn, had lain unnoticed by the scientific world until rediscovered in 1900. Previously, in the days when Fleeming Jenkin wrote, it was generally accepted that the then so-called theory of blending inheritance would govern individual variations; this may be briefly stated thus: the inheritance received by each individual came more or less equally from the two parents and that of the parents, of course, from their parents, and so on, with the different characters possessed by each member of a mating couple being blended together in the offspring. This idea had been expressed by Galton as the Law of Ancestral Inheritance which could be summarized by saying that the sum of the inherited qualities possessed by any individual could be regarded as having been derived on an average as follows:

$\frac{1}{2}$ of the total from the 2 parents
$\frac{1}{4}$ of the total from the 4 grandparents
$\frac{1}{8}$ of the total from the 8 great-grandparents
$\frac{1}{16}$ of the total from the 16 great-great-grandparents
                    . . . and so on to infinity

or it could be expressed as an equation of inheritance thus:

$$\frac{1}{2}p + \frac{1}{4}gp + \frac{1}{8}ggp + \frac{1}{16}gggp \ldots = I$$

where p, gp, ggp, gggp stand for parents, grandparents, great-grandparents, etc.

If such a theory was accepted (as it was at that time, but, of course, no longer held today) then it would seem impossible for Darwinism to work. As soon as some new favourable variety cropped up, it would be most unlikely for such an individual to come across and mate with another new sort of individual of the same kind. Thus in the next generation, half of the advantage of the new type would be blended away, and it would be still further reduced by a half in the following generation and so on, as seen in fig. 10. It seemed that any new variety must be blended away by the then accepted rules of inheritance long before selection could possibly operate to make it spread in the population. This criticism affected Darwin deeply and there can be little doubt that it made him, as we have seen (p. 69), introduce Lamarck's theory of use and disuse into his sixth and last edition of the *Origin* published in 1872, so much to Wallace's disapproval.

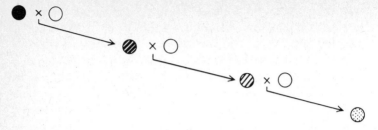

10. Diagram to show how (before the rediscovery of Mendel's laws) inheritance was thought (erroneously) to be of a blending type. The effect of a new variation (black circle) in a normal population would soon be blended away as its offspring bred with normal individuals (white circles) in subsequent generations.
From *The Living Stream*, p. 80.

Looking at *The Life and Letters of Charles Darwin*, Vol. III, edited by his son Francis, we see not only how upset he was, but how muddled he was in his correspondence with Wallace; writing to him on 2 February 1869 Darwin, in referring to an earlier letter, says:

> I must have expressed myself atrociously; I meant to say exactly the reverse of what you have understood. F. Jenkin argued . . . against single variations ever being perpetuated, and has convinced me, though not in quite so broad a manner as here put. I always thought individual differences more important; but I was blind and thought that single variations might be preserved much oftener than I now see is possible or probable. I mentioned this in my former note merely because I believed that you had come to a similar conclusion, and I like much to be in accord with you. I believe I was mainly deceived by single variations offering such simple illustrations, as when man selects.

You will recall (p. 66) that Osborn, in pointing out the difference between the original accounts of the theory of natural selection written by Darwin and Wallace, says 'Darwin dwells upon variations in single characters as taken hold of by selection, whereas Wallace is more concerned with *full formed varieties* as being favourably or unfavourably adapted.'

Now in 1885, three years after Darwin's death Weismann (1834–1914) dealt what appeared to be a crushing blow to Lamarckism with the publication of his *Theory of the Germ Plasm*. His idea was that the germ plasm, i.e. the part of the organism which is destined to give rise to the reproductive cells and so to the next generation, is usually isolated from the rest of the body at a very early stage in development. The substance of these future reproductive cells remains in a relatively unspecialized condition, so that an egg, which has been fertilized by the sperm cell, is able to give rise to a whole new individual; it divides and divides again, and the products go on dividing to build up a body of perhaps a hundred millions cells (as in man). Some of these cells are, as I have just said, put on one side and will form the ovary or testes which will provide the future reproductive cells; the rest, going on dividing, become specialized for different functions and form the nerve, muscle, gland, epithelial and other cells of the body. For Weismann, the specialized body is just the perambulator for carrying the baby, i.e. the germ plasm, which will be handed on to the next generation (fig. 11); it is this precious plasm which is potentially immortal. As far as we know, it has continued from far back in time for some two thousand million years. The body, which has become

11. A diagram to illustrate Weismann's conception of the continuity of the germ plasm (the blacked-in circles connected by a line) and its early separation from the body cells of the individuals which, having divided off from it, become specialized and will eventually die. The bodies die, but the germ plasm goes on and is potentially immortal.

89

specialized as a carrier, wears out; the price of such specialization is death. Generation after generation of such bodies are cast aside as the precious stream flows on. It does not matter, said Weismann, how much a body may enlarge this or that part by exercise, such changes cannot affect the germ plasm which has already been set on one side from the rest of the body. The effects of use or disuse could not be inherited. The stretching of a neck could not lead to a longer neck in the next generation; a duck (fig. 12) by stretching cannot eventually become a swan. Lamarckism appeared dead. Actually Weismann's theory is not completely true; it does not apply to plants or indeed to many animals such as flatworms, polyps and earthworms which can regenerate germ cells from body tissue. The criticism made by Jenkin, which had so much upset Darwin seemed either to have been forgotten or never really taken up.

With Weismann's apparent dismissal of Lamarckism Darwin's doctrine seemed supreme, with chance variations as the material upon which selection worked. Now it was that Charles Darwin's cousin, Francis Galton, began his detailed study of variation; he set about collecting all kinds of natural objects and measured the differences in their size, weight and

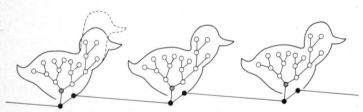

12. The same diagram as in fig. 11 but with the outline of the bodies of succeeding generations filled in. However much a duck, as an individual, might increase the length of its neck by continual stretching after food on the bottom of the pond, any such increase would not be passed on to the next generation because the germ cells had already been separated from the body cells at an early stage in development.

From *The Living Stream*, p. 76.

mending it as interesting reading 'to take no notice of his theories'. It was certainly Lyell's theories that had a profound influence on Darwin's thoughts; perhaps they may have had a greater effect on him than he himself actually realized, as I think we shall see.

Lyell's great merit was that he brought the geologists back to the pioneer views of Hutton (1736–97), who is often called the father of modern geology, and developed them much further. Hutton had been not only the first to demonstrate the volcanic origin of many rocks but also showed the effects of erosion, the carving out of valleys by rivers and the action of the sea; he showed the history of the earth to be a continuous natural process. These views had come in for strong criticism by the so-called 'catastrophists' who then ruled the day and believed the history of the world had been dominated by a series of catastrophies of which Noah's flood was considered to be the most recent. Lyell convinced the geologists that Hutton had been right and that the formation of the various layers of the rocks forming the earth's crust was indeed due to a succession of natural causes. Certainly Darwin was impressed and the realization of this long continuous process in the history of the earth prepared the way for his future thoughts on a continuous process of evolution; it is possible, however, that Lyell's book had an even more direct effect.

Many people have supposed that Lyell was not an evolutionist until he read Darwin's account of his theory; this, however, was not so, as was clearly indicated in Professor Judd's delightful little book *The Coming of Evolution* (Cambridge University Press, 1910). In Lyell's *Life and Letters* we see that whilst Darwin was still away on the *Beagle* he wrote to John Herschel in 1836 as follows:

> In regard to the origination of new species, I am very glad to find that you think it probable that it may be carried on through the intervention of intermediate causes. I left this rather to be inferred, not thinking it

worth while to offend a certain class of persons by embodying in words what would only be a speculation . . . One can in imagination summon before us a small part at least of the circumstances that must be contemplated and foreknown, before it can be decided what powers and qualities a new species must have in order to enable it to endure for a given time, and to play its part in due relation to all other beings destined to co-exist with it, before it dies out.

A year later, before Darwin had put forward his theory, he (Lyell) wrote to Whewell thus:

It was impossible, I think, for anyone to read my work and not to perceive that my notion of uniformity in the existing causes of change always implied that they must for ever produce an endless variety of effects, *both in the animate and inanimate world*.

Although Lyell never mentions evolution he was clearly an evolutionist before Darwin and there can be little doubt that, at any rate sub-consciously, the reading of the *Principles of Geology* prepared the ground for the growth of Darwin's thoughts.

There were two outstanding experiences during his voyage on the *Beagle* which set Darwin thinking along his evolutionary lines and a third one which, whilst not at once suggesting such a theory, was greatly to enrich his later thoughts about the process. During his stay in Patagonia he took part in some of the excavations of the fossil remains of those huge land sloths of the past such as *Mylodon* and also the giant armadillo-like animal *Glyptodon*; he recognized the essential similarity between the arrangement of the bones of the former and those in the skeleton of the much smaller modern tree sloths and again between those of *Glyptodon* and the modern armadillos. Could it be possible, he wondered, that the modern forms were descended from the same stock as the extinct ones? Then with even greater effect he saw how the entitled *Experiments in Plant Hybridisation* was read to the Brünn Natural History Society on 8 February 1865 and, as I have said, published in the same year. In the opening sentences of the first paper he says he had been at work for eight years 'on an experimental study of *evolution*'; that would be from the year before Darwin's and Wallace's first papers were published. He explains the care necessary in determining 'the number of different forms under which the offspring of hybrids appear or to arrange these forms with certainty according to their separate generations or to definitely ascertain their statistical relations'. He goes on:

> It requires indeed some courage to undertake a labour of such far-reaching extent: it appears, however, to be the only right way by which we can finally reach the solution of a question, the importance of which cannot be over-estimated in connection with the history of the evolution of organic forms.
>
> The paper now presented records the results of such a detailed experiment. This experiment was practically confined to a small plant group, and is now, after eight years' pursuit, concluded in all essentials. Whether the plan, upon which the separate experiments were conducted and carried out, was the best suited to attain the desired end is left to the friendly decision of the reader.

There can be little doubt that Mendel expected his labours would have been acclaimed by the scientific world; instead, they were almost completely ignored and he died nineteen years later, at the age of 62, a bitterly disappointed man. And sixteen years after his death he became world famous.

I must not turn this chapter into a treatise in elementary genetics; however, since neo-Darwinism *is* the fusion of Darwinian selection with Mendelian heredity, and its molecular-biological developments, it is essential that the reader should have some idea of what Mendelism stands for. Those who are familiar with Mendel's principles may skip a few pages, although they may like to look at p. 99 where they may be introduced to something about Mendel and his results that they never knew. Mendel, as you will remember, chose to study those characters of the pea which he found might each be in one or other of two forms: their seeds might be round or wrinkled, their flowers red or white, their stems tall or dwarf and so on; and when he crossed, say, round with wrinkled or tall with dwarf, he got all round seeded or all tall plants in the first generation and on crossing *these* he got round or wrinkled seeds, or tall or dwarf plants, roughly in the ratio of 3 : 1 in the next generation. It was as a result of many different carefully controlled crosses and back crosses, by using algebra, and by assuming that the factor for tallness was dominant over that for dwarfness, round seed dominant to wrinkled, etc., that he concluded that for each of the many different kinds of characters there must be a pair of factors responsible. In his first and most important law he said that at the formation of the reproductive cells (ovule or pollen grain in plants), the two members of such a pair of factors segregate so that each reproductive cell has one member of each kind of pair. Today, of course, we call such a unit factor a gene. At the union of the reproductive cells to form the next generation the pair of genes are restored, one coming from each parent. I give a simple diagram which illustrates his first law, and the following brief description merely to remind those who may now have forgotten what they learnt long ago.

In the diagram in fig. 14 showing the crossing of a tall pea with a dwarf pea, the 'T's' represent the factors for tallness, and the 't's' the factors for dwarfness. Now as these segregate to give single representatives in the ovules or pollen grains, then a factor for tallness *must* mate with a factor for dwarfness to give the constitution 'Tt' in the first generation. Tallness being dominant over dwarfness, each of these 'Tt' plants will be tall. Now on crossing such plants each will have two kinds of ovules or pollen grains, half carrying 'T' and half 't', so that each 'T' has an equal chance of combining with either another 'T' or with a 't' (similarly each 't' can combine equally with either) giving us in the next generation 'TT', 'Tt' and 'tt', but with the chance of there being twice as many 'Tt's as of the other two kinds. This gives us the well known ratio of 3 : 1, i.e. 3 tall to 1 dwarf – of which the tall ones are of two kinds, one being what we call homozygous, being 'TT', and the others being heterozygous, being 'Tt'.

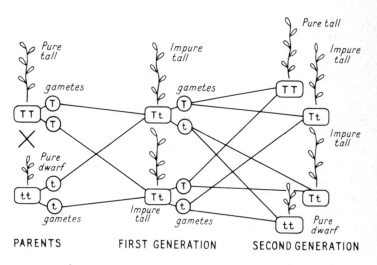

14. An example of the working of Mendel's first law as applied to plants; for explanation see text.
From *The Living Stream*, p. 85.

I here give in tabular form the actual results that Mendel published showing how he dealt with various kinds of variation such as seed form, flower position, height of stem, etc. The figures show the numbers of the different kinds of plants he got in the *second* generation after crossing one type of plant with the other, and in the third column we see the ratio which of course is never exactly 3 : 1, but very near it.

TABLE III

A summary of Mendel's results

	Dominant	Recessive	Ratio
Seed form	5474 round	1850 wrinkled	2·96 : 1
Cotyledon colour	6022 yellow	2001 green	3·01 : 1
Seed-coats, form	882 inflated	299 wrinkled	2·95 : 1
Seed-coats, colour	705 grey	224 white	3·15 : 1
Unripe pods, colour	428 green	152 yellow	2·82 : 1
Flower position	651 axial	207 terminal	3·14 : 1
Stem	787 tall	277 dwarf	2·84 : 1
	14,949 (74.9%)	5010 (25.1%)	2·98 : 1 or 3 : 1

I am giving these figures because in a moment I want to say something about them which perhaps is not known to many outside biological circles.

The characters which were studied by Mendel and all the workers in animal genetics in the early days were naturally the rather more striking characters, such as red and white flowers, or black and normal fruit flies, etc., and it was shown that it was such characters which from time to time suddenly appeared as if from nowhere. They were what gardeners had long called 'sports', and it was these which they bred from to give us the new kinds of garden flowers; and it was the same with animals. Suddenly a different type appears and, if bred from, will be found to obey Mendel's laws. This indeed fitted well with de Vries's theory. Evolution was now thought by most biologists to be proceeding by these sudden jumps or mutations, with selection playing but a minor role: a mere pruning knife, as it were, instead of the great creative force the Darwinians had supposed it to be. This, however, was only short-lived.

Very soon after the rediscovery of Mendel's laws, it was realized how very similar was the supposed behaviour of his hereditary factors to that of the bodies called the chromosomes, long thread-like bodies in the nucleus of each cell, which had been shown to occur in pairs. As the reproductive cells are formed, there is a particular kind of cell division, called meiosis, in which the chromosomes, after coming together in their pairs, separate so that each future egg or sperm, ovule or pollen grain, will have only one of each kind. At first it was thought that the chromosomes themselves might actually be these factors but soon it was shown that there were many more Mendelian factors than there were chromosomes. It was the great T. H. Morgan in America, with his brilliant team of co-workers, who founded and developed the chromosomal theory of the gene, showing that the Mendelian factors or genes, as he now called them, lie in the chromosomes; and then he further proved by a remarkable and elaborate technique of breeding that they lie in a *linear order* along the chromosomes. As all will know, the Morgan school mapped the actual positions of the different genes along the chromosomes of the little fruit fly *Drosophila*.

I now come to an extraordinary little item in our story discovered by the late Sir Ronald Fisher. It is the surprising fact that according to the laws of statistics, the ratios which Mendel published as the result of his experiments appear far too good to be true; never in the history of experimental breeding have such a series of ratios consistently been so near the 3 : 1 figures his theory demanded. Everywhere where Mendel's laws have been tested they have been found to be correct, yet it appears that the detailed figures for the results he first published could never have been true, or at least could only have been true by what one might describe as an absolute miracle of chance. Fisher, perhaps our greatest biological statistician, says, after a lengthy examination,[1] that it is inconceivable that such ratios could have been obtained. I do not think that anyone supposes that Mendel himself deliberately faked the results. It seems most likely

---

[1] R. A. Fisher (1936). Has Mendel's work been rediscovered? *Annals of Science*, vol. I. (See his p. 132 onwards.)

that – and this, as Fisher suggests, perhaps makes Mendel an even greater figure than one hitherto thought, – instead of his first doing a vast number of experiments and *then* coming to his conclusion, he, after a few trials, worked out his theory by mathematics in his study and then put it to the test. One can imagine him telling his gardeners of his theory, why he was doing the experiments, and why he expected to get a ratio close to, but not exactly, 3 : 1. As the experiments proceeded, the gardeners who helped him no doubt saw quite clearly that the results were coming out as he had foretold; and, assisting in the counting, it must be supposed that they saved themselves much trouble by giving Mendel the results as he had foretold, not exactly but very nearly 3 : 1 – too near as it turned out! With painstaking care Mendel himself no doubt carried out the pollinations but perhaps left the mere counting to his assistants. We shall never know the exact truth behind this story.

At first few people seemed to realize that Mendel's demonstration that inheritance was of a particulate nature instead of the old blending type gave back to the Darwinian doctrine what it wanted to make it work. A new favourable variety, instead of being blended away in the coming generations, is just shuffled backwards and forwards, generation after generation, without being changed until there comes the rare event of mutation. In fig. 15 we see how the Mendelian factors are being thrown to and fro between the members of the population at each generation without diminishing their unit values; the diagram, for clarity, however, shows just *one pair* of such factors, whereas actually there are thousands continually being brought together in different combinations.

It was some time before most biologists realized that the objections to Darwinian theory had now been removed. Even as late as 1936 at a special symposium organized by the Royal Society to consider 'The Present State of the Theory of Natural Selection' considerable doubt was expressed by a number of speakers as to whether selection was really the all

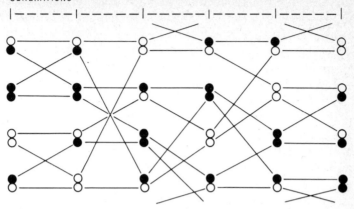

15. A diagram showing the flow of mendelian factors (the genes) in a population from generation to generation; only a single pair of factors is shown whereas there may be thousands being transmitted in a continuous reassortment. Compare this with the old idea of blending inheritance shown in fig. 10 (p. 88); here there is no dilution of the effects of a new variation.
From *The Living Stream*, p. 90.

important agent. It was only after much more genetical breeding had been accomplished, together with a fuller appreciation of the brilliant mathematical studies of the power of selection made by Sir Ronald Fisher in his classic work *The Genetical Theory of Natural Selection*, which he had published in 1930, that Darwinism came into its own again, but now firmly linked with Mendelism.

The great developments of evolutionary theory in the present century lie in the field of genetics. In this brief survey I can only touch on a few of the important points. We have seen that from time to time a gene undergoes a change – a mutation – whereby its effect upon inheritance is altered. These changes are more likely to be harmful than beneficial and the former are continually being eliminated. To be effective these mutations must be relatively rare events. Schrödinger makes an interesting comparison with the industrial world. He says if a works manager wants to improve the efficiency of his factory, he will make only one change at a time, otherwise he would not know which one is bringing about the desired effect; so also, he says, too high a mutation rate in nature would defeat the evolutionary ends. Unstable genes – those that mutate too easily – will tend to be eliminated from the system by natural selection.

It was thought at first, as it was by Mendel, that there was a unit factor (or gene, as we now say) governing each particular character of an animal or plant; now, however, we realize that the effects which we are seeing are the result of the interaction of vast numbers of such genes. Whilst each particular gene may have a more pronounced effect upon one part of the body than another (and so becomes labelled as the gene for this or that), it is really producing many other effects; both structually and physiologically. One gene which may influence the colour of part of an animal may also be making it more tolerant of extremes of temperature, humidity, etc. We know now that genes may have effects in both space and time, i.e. some may govern the rates of development of different parts of the body of an organism, so that one part may appear earlier or later than usual in the course of development. Above all we now realize that all these different effects are acting together to create a joint genetical influence: what we call today *the gene complex*. The appearance of any organism is the product of this internal gene complex interacting with the external environment in which it has been brought up.

I must not become too technical, but I think the reader will like to have just a glimpse of the complex inter-relationships between Darwinian selection and Mendelian heredity in the modern development of the neo-Darwinian position. Following the concept of the gene complex, it came to be realized that the *effect* of any mutant gene may be more beneficial – or more harmful – in one gene complex than in another. In no two individuals, except identical twins, will the gene complex be exactly the same; so great is the number of possible different combinations of genes that it is inconceivable on statistical grounds that they could be the same.[2] Since the general appearance of an organism is the result of the combined action of *all* its genes, it follows that the *effect* of *any particular one* will depend in some degree upon the united action of the others. This leads to the important concept that the *effect* of any gene *is subject to genetic variation*; i.e. not the gene itself, but *its effect* may be altered by changes, mutations and recombinations in the rest of the gene complex. This, therefore, means that the *effect* of a gene is *subject to selection*. The reality of this is seen in the improvement in the viability of a new mutant form after several generations of inbreeding; those individuals whose complex reacts unfavourably are eliminated.

There is so much more that could be said about the modern concept of the gene complex, but I must confine myself to only one more point. So nicely balanced is the complex in relation to the external environment that only very rarely can we expect a new mutation to be an improvement. For the same reason it is the mutations *with very small effects* that are most likely to be successful in improving the stock; a big or violent change is most likely to be harmful.

We realize how far we are now from the conception that de Vries put forward at the beginning of the century. Instead of evolution proceeding, as he thought, by big jumps – almost new species bounding into existence with selection playing little or no part in their production – we see what are usually tiny changes developing under the influence of selection, little steps far below the species level of difference. We are brought back to Darwinism, the action of natural selection upon small inherited variations; but it is Darwinism with an important difference; that of particulate inheritance.

To understand the present-day position of the neo-Darwinian theory we must come to a consideration of the nature of the genes themselves. The chromosomes carrying

[2] R. A. Fisher: *The Genetical Theory of Natural Selection*, 1930; also T. Dobzhansky: *Genetics and the Origin of Species*, 1937.

the genes have the remarkable power of reduplicating themselves in the process of cell division called mitosis, which goes on repeatedly during the growth of an individual; by this means the genetic elements are distributed in exactly equal quantities, without change, to all the cells of the body. When the time for reproduction comes, however, we see a significant modification of this process as the sexual cells are being formed.

Sex is that fundamental evolutionary device for bringing about the re-assortment of the genes as one generation follows another. It is in the preparation (or in the maturation as we say) of the germ cells for reproduction that a change in the form of cell division comes into play: the process called meiosis which halves the number of chromosomes in the resulting reproductive cells. We now realize that this division (a kind of telescoped double mitosis) does something much more than this. It is itself a product of evolution ensuring that any new mutant genes are spread through the population and tried out in different genetical combinations with all possible speed. It is a device for increasing variability: a special mechanism for shuffling the genes.

Instead of the chromosomes just coming together in pairs before division, as was originally thought, they twist round one another in pairing and in so doing break, so that corresponding parts of a pair of chromosomes are interchanged and joined up together again. One chromosome which, before pairing, may have had say, genes A, G, L and T at intervals along its length, may be changed to have A, g, L and t at the end of the process, g and t having come in with those parts of the other chromosome, with which it paired and twisted, in exchange for the parts carrying G and T.

Parallel with these advances in our knowledge of cell mechanics came all the wonderful discoveries of the biochemists regarding the materials of which plant and animal bodies are made. Reproduction and growth are among the most characteristic properties of living things, and naturally both can only be brought about by the production of new material similar to the old; the many different complex chemical substances of the body must be duplicated.

The capacity for growth and reproduction is astonishing. The continual biochemical multiplication of material, coupled with the organisms' sexual drive for reproduction, produces the colossal pressure which not only forces life into every niche that will receive it, but makes the process of selective survival absolutely inevitable. The corollary is, of course, clear enough for man; unless the world controls its reproductive rate, a deadly struggle for survival must ensue: one which might turn out to be not one of survival but of extinction.

Several authors had put forward reasons for believing that the gene was a complex chemical molecule. This was well argued by H. J. Müller in his Pilgrim Trust Lecture to the Royal Society, entitled 'The Gene', in 1945; independently it was also the main theme of the very remarkable little book *What is Life?* (already referred to on p. 40) by that great physicist, the late Erwin Schrödinger, published in 1944. Schrödinger was perhaps the first to suggest how the atomic variations in such large molecules could provide a basic code for specifying the most detailed 'information' governing the step by step stages in the development of an individual. Slight changes in the atomic arrangement of a molecule – a mutation – would mean an alteration in the specification which would change the resulting organism. As he pointed out, a code, like the morse code, using just two signs, dot and dash, in groups of not more than four: e.g.

$$— \cdot, \cdot —, — \cdot —, \cdot \cdot —, — \cdot — \cdot, — \cdot \cdot —, \text{ etc.}$$

can give 30 different specifications. If three signs were used, say $\cdot$, — and $\times$, and in groups of not more than ten, they would give 29,524 different specifications; and if five signs were used, say $\cdot$, —, $\times$, o and +, in groups of not more than 25 there would be 372,529,029,846,191,405 different specifications!

It might be argued, Schrödinger said, that this is a bad analogy with the genetic material because in such a total we are including groups of different numerical composition, as: —·, —··—, etc. To remedy this defect, he said, we could pick from the last example only the combinations of exactly 25 symbols and only those containing exactly five of each of the separate types, for example:

```
·····   —————   ×××××   ooooo   +++++   ·×——·
·+o—o   ××·++   o+o×·   ——+×o   —·—×o   ++×··
·—oo—   ×+×+—   ·oo×+
```
etc.

A rough calculation now gives 62,000,000,000,000 such alternatives; this gives plenty of scope for a most detailed specification of development and there are many more than 25 genes.

These suggestions have indeed turned out to be true. The genetic code *is* in the form of a giant molecule which is called for short the DNA; its nature was discovered and worked out by the two Nobel prizewinners F. H. C. Crick and J. D. Watson in 1955 working together at Cambridge. To explain the nature of DNA I shall have to be somewhat technical. DNA is short for deoxyribonucleic acid, but we need not bother with its full name in this simple account except that we should distinguish it from another nucleic acid which is ribonucleic acid or RNA for short. The difference between them is that the sugar molecules that are built into them are what are called ribose sugars, one of which lacks an atom of oxygen that is present in the other, so that it is called deoxy-ribose sugar, giving us the long full name of the DNA. I shall refer to the RNA presently; it is the DNA, however, which gives us the genetic code and occurs only in the nucleus of the cell, in fact only in the chromosomes.

To understand the form of the DNA molecule, first imagine two long chains each made up of phosphate and sugar molecules linked together thus: phosphate – sugar – phosphate – sugar . . . alternating for thousands of times.

Now, for a moment, imagine them to be parallel to one another like the two sides of a ladder with rungs made up of two chemicals called bases linking together the sugars of the two sides of the ladder as shown in the diagram in fig. 16; I have just said 'for a moment' imagine them thus, for actually the ladder is twisted to form the famous double helix. The two sides of the ladder spiral round one another as if they

```
        \                           /
    SUGAR — BASE — BASE — SUGAR
      /                           \
PHOSPHATE                     PHOSPHATE
        \                       /
    SUGAR — BASE — BASE — SUGAR
      /                           \
PHOSPHATE                     PHOSPHATE
        \                       /
    SUGAR — BASE — BASE — SUGAR
      /                           \
PHOSPHATE                     PHOSPHATE
        \                       /
    SUGAR — BASE — BASE — SUGAR
      /                           \
PHOSPHATE                     PHOSPHATE
        \                       /
    SUGAR — BASE — BASE — SUGAR
      /                           \
PHOSPHATE                     PHOSPHATE
        \                       /
    SUGAR — BASE — BASE — SUGAR
      /                           \
```

were one above the other on the surface of a vertical cylinder with the rungs (the bases) connecting one with the other *horizontally* (geometrically like the chords in a circle) within the cylinder as I have endeavoured to show in the simplified diagram in fig. 17.

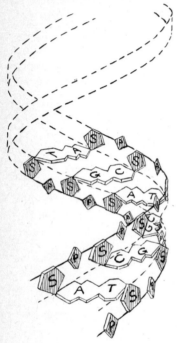

17. A simplified diagram of the double helix of the DNA molecule. The two side chains spiral round one above the other as on the surface of a cylinder, but the connecting links are horizontal and geometrically form chords across the inside of the cylinder. The parts marked S and P represent the sugar and phosphate units and A, T, G and C represent the bases adenine, thymine, guanine and cytosine respectively.

Now the substances called 'bases' linking together the two sides of the molecule like the rungs of a ladder are of four kinds, and they are always linked together in just two kinds of pairs:

Adenine linked to Thymine
Guanine linked to Cytosine

So the connecting 'rungs' may be adenine-thymine, thymine-adenine, guanine-cytosine, cytosine-guanine and, in their thousands in a single molecule, they may be arranged in any order. It is now known that it is the almost endless possible combinations and permutations of these pairs which provide the code system.

We must now consider how the DNA molecules are able to reduplicate themselves at every division of the nucleus and so pass on the code unchanged (except for the rare accidents that give us mutations) to every cell of the body. Crick and Watson put forward a hypothesis to suggest how this might be done and it has now been shown to be true. The two sides of the double helix of the DNA untwist and come apart, like the two sides of a zip fastener, separating at the links between the two pairs of bases as shown in the diagram in fig. 18. Each side chain now picks up from the nuclear plasm new units (each a base with sugar and phosphate attached) of the appropriate kind to fit the bases along its length: i.e. an adenine sector always picks up a thymine unit, a cytosine sector always picks up a guanine unit and so on. Thus each separate half of the original molecule will build up a new part corresponding exactly to the half to which it was formerly linked; in place of one DNA molecule we now have two exactly the same. So it is that the genetic code comes to every part of the individual's body as it is built up in development – cell division after cell division – from the fertilized egg.

I will now just refer again to that other nucleic acid RNA which I mentioned on p. 106. It is the RNA which acts as the go-between of the genetic code of the DNA and the production of the almost infinite number of different kinds of proteins necessary for the building up of the body during development. This carries us into the fields of advanced bio-chemistry and physiology which cannot be a part of this book. I need only say that these proteins vary one from another by an even greater array of possible combinations and permutations than those in the code of the DNA; this extraordinary range of possible variation is provided by *twenty* different kinds of amino-acid units which may be linked together in all sorts of ways and sequences in their hundreds of thousands to build the great protein molecules.

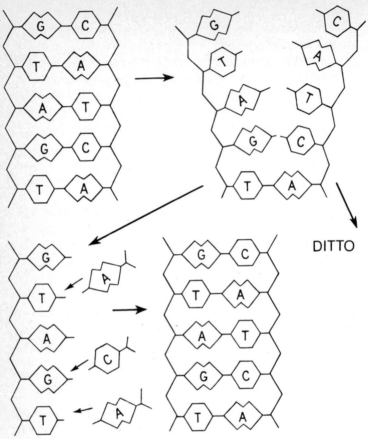

DITTO

18. Diagrams to illustrate the reduplication of the DNA molecule according to the views of Watson and Crick. For explanation see text.

As Crick has said, 'The genetic code is the dictionary which relates the four-letter language of the DNA with the twenty-letter language of the proteins.'

Now here is something that closely links up with what we have been saying about the continuous chemical activity in the evolutionary stream of life, for it is remarkable that there is little or no essential difference in the general form of the DNA molecules at different stages in this long organic history from the lowest organisms to man; it is only the details of their coding arrangements that are different. Even in bacteria the system is essentially the same.

This brief sketch will, I think, suffice to show that we can no longer doubt that the bodily variations upon which natural selection acts are indeed chemical in nature; they are due on the one hand to accidents in the reduplication of the DNA molecules producing mutations and, on the other, to the continual shuffling and recombinations of such novelties with the other genetic elements in the population by sexual reproduction with its preparatory meiotic divisions. I fully accept the material mechanism of this process; whilst our knowledge of its details will no doubt be modified in the future, its general chemical nature cannot be doubted with the evidence now before us.

All this chemistry is wonderful, exciting and brilliant science, but as I hope to show later in the book, it does not take us to the very heart of the nature of life or tell us more than only a part of the evolution story. Dr Crick who has done so much to reveal these wonders to us ends an article[3] which he wrote in 1957 with these words: 'From every point of view biology is getting nearer and nearer to the molecular level. Here in the realm of heredity we now find ourselves dealing with polymers [i.e. chain molecules] and reducing the decisive controls of life to a matter of the precise order in which monomers [i.e. the units in a chain] are arranged in a giant molecule.' He talks of 'the decisive controls of life' and many people follow him in this belief; we shall see, however, that it is a fallacy.

Certainly the genetic code, together with the effects of the environment which are not inherited, appear to be governing the form of the individual's *physical* body, but equally certainly it is *not* governing the course of evolution; it is sup-

---

[3] *The Scientific American*, September 1957.

plying the almost infinite range of variation within any population of animals and plants upon which natural selection acts. It is selection that guides the process of evolution and, as we shall see, selection is far from random; there are, moreover, many different kinds of selection, and some of them, I believe, have not so far been recognized. We have not come to the end of neo-Darwinism, for we do not yet understand the nature of consciousness, nor the part it may play in the process.

6

The Creative Power of Natural Selection

There are many different kinds of natural selection. Two are obvious: selection by the physical environment and that by the animate world, the action of predators and competitors in the struggle for life. Examples are endless; of the former we all know that mammals with thicker fur tend to survive better in polar climates than those with thinner coats, or flightless insects tend to be found on oceanic islands for the simple reason that those with wings are more likely to be carried off the island by the wind than those without them. As for the action of predators, it is the fastest runners of their prey that tend to survive and show us the evolution of the magnificent powers of locomotion of the antelopes, deer and horses; and indeed it is the fastest of the predators which get sufficient food to survive and give us such high speed runners as the cheetah. The action of competitors leads to the selection of those better equipped for gathering food where the supply is limited or for winning the necessary territory for breeding sites. We see the power of selection everywhere.

In this chapter I want to show how 'creative' natural selection can be; we shall see it affecting not only bodily form, but sometimes also producing at the same time instinctive behaviour to go with it. I must make these elements of more normal selection quite clear before going on in the next chapter to discuss examples of what I believe to be a form of selection of a very different kind.

Now before discussing selection in general, I should mention that there is yet another particular kind which is by no means always favourable to the race. It was, I believe, Professor J. B. S. Haldane who first pointed this out in 1932 in his book *Causes of Evolution* when he spoke of the fallacy of assuming that the action of natural selection must *always* make a race of animals and plants fitter in its struggle with the environment. He described it as 'a fallacy which has been responsible for a good deal of poisonous nonsense which has been written on ethics in Darwin's name, especially in Germany before the war and in America and England since'. He was of course referring to the first world war and writing just before Hitler came to power. He clearly showed that there are many subtle ways in which competition between members of the same species may lead to the selection of features that eventually must spell ruin to the race. Some of these features, however, are more obvious, such as the weapons evolved for combat between rivals of their own kind. 'The geological record,' as Haldane says, 'is full of cases where the development of enormous horns and spines (sometimes in the male sex only) has been the prelude to extinction. It seems probable,' he continues, 'that in some of these cases the species literally sank under the weight of its own armaments.' It is indeed a lesson for mankind today.

In order to show up the 'creative' powers of natural selection I am going to devote this chapter to a study of adaptive coloration in animals. In doing so I will use a number of the original drawings which I made for the same purpose in my book *The Living Stream* which has long been out of print; I shall also reproduce a good deal of the text, for I feel I cannot improve the argument by expressing it in another form. I make no apology for dealing with this form of adaptation again, for to my mind it brings out features in the process, such as the combination of colour patterns and distinctive behaviour which cannot be demonstrated so clearly in any other similar study.

Before coming to some of these remarkable effects I will briefly describe two series of beautifully designed experiments which show us the actual operation of selection in bringing them about. The first are those of Dr E. J. Popham who studied the colour variations in that common aquatic insect, the water-boatman,[1] so-called because of its pair of long oar-like legs with which it rows itself rapidly through the water. He published his findings in the *Proceedings of the Zoological Society of London in* 1941. Having noticed while collecting round Richmond that most of the specimens closely resembled the colour of the ponds they were swimming in and, finding that other naturalists had made similar observations, he decided to make an experimental study of it. Using a standard colour chart he made a scale of greys passing in stages from light to dark which he labelled *a* to *p* and which had increasing percentages of black in them. In judging the colour of the insects he collected, he held them in glass tubes against the colour scale and recorded between which two shades their colour lay. Similarly he judged the colour of the bottoms of the different ponds by viewing them against his colour scale when looking vertically down into them. He found that in the nine different ponds he studied, which varied widely in colour, the majority of the insects in each corresponded in colour to their background. I am not giving all his tables of percentages; they can be found in his paper. He then found that the insects had become provided with instinctive colour preferences; by keeping them in aquaria with strips of different greys on the bottom he showed that the different insects more often than not tended to rest on the background which they matched. He now made his striking experiments in the actual operation of selection by using small fish, rudd, as predators; by putting equal numbers of insects of colour *i* and *l* on his scale into an aquarium with an *i* background and replacing, by others of the same kind, those insects that were eaten, until a total of 200 had been taken, he found that 151 of the darker colour had been taken as against only 49 of those matching their

[1] *Arctocorisa distincta.*

background. Again, using fish in four separate aquaria which had background colours of *a*, *c*, *e*, and *g* respectively, he experimented with 9 insects at a time having always 3 of each colour *n*, *l* and *i* present (i.e. by at once replacing those eaten). He continued until 100 insects had been taken in each aquarium. Here I will introduce one of his tables for it will make the results clearer than a long written account:

Table of Percentage of different insects taken in each experiment

	n	*l*	*i*
Experiment with background *a*	33	34	33
Experiment with background *c*	36	38	26
Experiment with background *e*	41	32	27
Experiment with background *g*	53	36	11

This shows clearly that it is the *contrast* between the colour of the insect and its background that determines its chances of being eaten or not. In the first experiment the three kinds of insects are all so different from their background that they are all equally likely to be taken. As we go down the series of experiments, the contrast between the insects and their background is getting less and less. In the last experiment, for example, insect *i* is only *one* stage in his scale of colour from its background, and only 11 per cent of those taken are of this shade as compared with 53 per cent of those coloured *n* which are *three* degrees on his scale away from the background. This is a brilliant demonstration of the force of predator selection in determining colour variation.

Space will only permit me to mention one more of his experiments, and here again I will use his table; this time demonstrating the relative average time taken by a fish to catch 24 insects in five different populations containing two different colour varieties *l* and *i*, in different relative proportions, each against an i background. The results were as follows:

	Number of insects coloured l	Number of insects coloured i	Average time taken to catch each of 24 insects
Experiment 1	24	0	22 secs.
2	18	6	31
3	12	12	39
4	6	18	45
5	0	24	48

We see how much more quickly an insect is caught when it differs from its background than when it is of the same shade.

If it be objected that these are really laboratory experiments and perhaps tell us something different from what is happening in the wild, no such criticism can be levelled against another piece of work I am about to describe. Here is a study of a widespread evolutionary change which we see actually taking place in our own day.

In 1848 a jet black variety, *carbonaria*, of the geometrid moth *Biston betularia* – the well-known salt-and-pepper moth – was first taken near Manchester, and before long other specimens of the same black form began to be taken in other such urban areas. During the latter part of the century, these black varieties were increasing in number throughout all the industrial regions of Britain and those on the continent as well, particularly in Germany. They were followed by black, or dark varieties of a number of other species of moths. It was very soon suggested that they might be produced by natural selection favouring the black forms against the more sooty backgrounds, but at first this was just laughed at, for few were ready to believe that the grime was so bad as to cause such an effect.

It was not until after the last war that an experimental study of industrial melanism, as the phenomenon came to be known, was tackled in earnest by Dr Bernard Kettlewell[2] at Oxford, who showed that it gave the most striking proof of the working of Darwinian natural selection under wild life conditions. He explored the problem from several different angles and from each approach the evidence fitted together in a most remarkable way. From a nation-wide survey he showed that the black varieties of *Biston betularia* occurred in large numbers through great tracts of country, not only in the immediate vicinities of industrial development, but also for some considerable distance to the east of such regions, where the prevailing winds were from the west. He also surveyed Great Britain for deposits of soot, taking rubbings from the trunks of trees and from their leaves, then plotting the distribution of contamination on a map. He showed that such areas of grime corresponded closely with the distribution of the black variety of this moth. It bears its English name of the salt-and-pepper moth because its wings have the appearance of being dusted irregularly with splashes of these condiments, a coloration which provides an excellent camouflage against the grey, irregular background of the typical lichen-covered tree trunks upon which it rests in the daytime. With its wings outspread, it presents a perfect imitation of the lichen effect. Now, as Kettlewell has shown, the typical lichen will not grow where the soot deposit exceeds a certain figure and here, on the blackened tree trunks, the typical salt-and-pepper coloration is extremely conspicuous, but the black form is almost invisible. In uncontaminated England, where the lichen still thrives, it is the black variety which is conspicuous. The contrast of the two situations is shown in fig. 19 in sketches I made from photographs.

For his experiments Kettlewell chose two contrasting scenes: the Cadbury Bournville estate, in the well-named

[2] H. B. D. Kettlewell, *Heredity*, vol. 9, pp. 323–42, 1955; *ibid*, vol. 10, pp. 287–301, 1956; *Proc. Royal Society*, Series B, vol. 145, pp. 297–303, 1956.

19. The salt-and-pepper moth, *Biston betularia*. *a*, the typical form; *b*, the black variety *carbonaria*; *c*, a drawing from a photograph of the two forms at rest on the lichen-covered bark of a tree, each being directly below its portrait above; *d*, the same two forms on the soot-darkened, lichen-free bark of a tree in a smoke-polluted area, also drawn from a photograph with the moths in exactly the same positions.

From *The Living Stream*, p. 121.

'Black Country' near Birmingham, and a completely unpolluted wood in Dorset. First of all he collected large numbers of this moth in the two areas. In the Bournville area the population was made up of 91 per cent black forms and 9 per cent normal type; in the Dorset wood his collection gave only 2 per cent of the black kind with 98 per cent of the typical salt-and-pepper pattern. The latter result shows us that this black mutation must be one which is occurring regularly in the wild populations. He now bred large quantities of both the black and normal kinds and marked each individual with a tiny spot of red quick-drying enamel on the underside of a wing, so that it would not be seen when the insect was at rest. He then liberated nearly a thousand on the Bourneville estate, in almost equal numbers of the black and normal types. After a week's time he set up his mercury vapour lamps (lamps which entomologists now use to attract moths for capture in large quantities) and recorded only the moths he caught bearing the little red identity labels showing that they were certainly ones which he had released. Of those he recaptured, 29 were black and only 11 were of the salt-and-pepper form; this clearly showed that the latter were being eliminated almost three times as quickly as the black. The same experiment was made in the Dorset woodland, giving almost exactly the opposite result: with only 5 of the black being recaught as against 16 of the normal type; clearly there is a distinct but opposite differential death rate between the two forms in the two areas.

Next, with the help of Dr Niko Tinbergen, he took a film showing this very act of selection going on. In the Dorset wood they set up their camera in a camouflaged hide and focused it on a tree trunk on which they placed 6 of these moths, 3 black and conspicuous, and 3 normal ones on the lichen background. So they watched and filmed the birds coming to take the moths; again and again in this remarkable record you see birds of several different species picking off the black *carbonaria*, and leaving the typical salt-and-pepper kinds. It is the most striking demonstration of Darwinian natural selection taking place before your eyes. In addition to taking the film, they kept watch in turns and recorded the relative numbers of each kind of moth taken and by the different species of bird. As moths were picked off, fresh specimens were put out on to the tree trunk to keep the numbers 3 of each kind; 164 black were taken as against 26 of the typical. In the Birmingham district the birds were seen to take 43 of the salt-and-pepper type (here conspicuous on the soot-blackened bark) and only 15 of the black variety.

The spread of this industrial melanism, an evolutionary change taking place over large areas within quite recent times, is here clearly shown to be produced by the action of natural selection upon the gene complex changing by mutation. Dr Kettlewell has now recorded a number of other refinements of the process of improving the black colouring in this and other species. Further, this form of selection has apparently not only controlled the proportions of the colour varieties in the different populations, but Kettlewell has found that there have developed in relation to this colour variation differences in the moths' instinctive behaviour. Just as Dr Popham had demonstrated with his differently coloured water-boatmen insects (p. 115), so Kettlewell has shown[3] that when the moths have a choice of a light or dark background on which to settle, the dark *carbonaria* variety, more often than not, tends to settle on the dark background rather than a light one, whereas for the lighter salt-and-pepper variety it is the opposite.

Similar proof of the force of selection in the field by predators was obtained by Dr A. J. Cain and Dr P. M. Sheppard when working at Oxford on the colour variations of the snail *Cepaea nemoralis*[4] and later by Dr B. C. Clarke for the allied species *C. hortensis*.[5] The experimental demonstration of selection has now accumulated fast. Dr Niko Tinbergen's school of Animal Behaviour at Oxford has shown the significance (in quantitative terms of selection) of such camouflage effects as counter-shading in some species of caterpillars, and the imitation of twigs in others, or in the frightening qualities of pronounced eye markings on the wings of many moths.[6] In the last-mentioned experiments

[3] *Nature*, vol. 175, p. 943 (1955).
[4] *Heredity*, vol. 4, pp. 275–94 (1950); *ibid.*, vol. 6, pp. 217–31 (1952), and *Genetics*, vol. 39, pp. 89–116 (1954).
[5] *Heredity*, vol. 14, pp. 423–43 (1960); *ibid.*, vol. 17, pp. 319–45 (1962).
[6] The experiments are well summarized in Dr Tinbergen's most attractive series of essays: *Curious Naturalists* (1958).

we see how birds will leave alone a moth which suddenly displays the alarming large eye pattern, almost like the eyes of an owl, whereas when the scales on the wings forming the eye pattern have been brushed off the moth is attacked and eaten with avidity.

Alfred Russel Wallace was the great pioneer in analysing animal and plant coloration in terms of natural selection in his *Tropical Nature* (1878) and *Darwinism* (1889), closely followed by Edward Poulton in his *The Colours of Animals* (1890); then came the Thayers' (A. H. and G. H.) *Concealing Coloration in the Animal Kingdom* (1909 and new edition 1918) and the magnificent monograph by H. B. Cott on *Adaptive Coloration in Animals* (1940). In spite of all that has been written, the subject has certain elements which have not, I believe, been sufficiently stressed and make it particularly appropriate for our discussion here.

First of all I will give examples of certain types of animal camouflage, or cryptic (concealing) colouring as we say in biology, and then touch on the opposite principle of warning coloration. It is interesting to compare animal camouflage with man's efforts in the same direction. Nature is incomparably superior to man in this. We see in both fields the same course of development with first of all the adoption of a general background colour, then a picking out of some particular feature in the landscape as a theme for a simple pattern, and finally an exact imitation of parts of the environment under special circumstances. I am speaking metaphorically; the animal itself is not picking out its colour scheme – that is the work of selection. We are all familiar with the general mottled appearance of moorland birds, the sandy colours of desert creatures or the snowy white of many Arctic animals. Man's first realization of the importance of such protection in war was the adoption of similar general background colours, like our own khaki or the neutral greys of the continental armies. We then see many animals with the main feature patterns: the tiger reproducing the black vertical shadows seen among the bright, sunlit dry bamboos of the jungle, or the leopard with his spotted coat invisible against the dappled sunshine and shadow under forest foliage, or, nearer home, the striped breast and the upward pointing beak of a bittern standing rigidly amongst the reeds when in danger. So man, following the same general course, has begun to develop a blotched battledress and mottled tents. Going further, the modern soldier conceals some of his fixed positions, observation posts or machine-gun emplacements by painting them to be exact imitations of a bit of hedge, a haystack or some other object of the countryside; in this, however, he is quite out-classed by many animals, particularly insects, which may spend part of the day at rest, as facsimile copies of leaves, twigs and other parts of plants. In fig. 20 I show drawings of two insects masquerading as leaves complete in such details as might be produced by an artist illustrating some botanical work; see also the leaf butterfly in fig. 28a (p. 130). These are the commonplace types of adaptive coloration; while perfect of their kind, they are not, to my mind, the most significant of nature's 'designs'.

The animal world covers the whole range of the artist's subtlety in producing effects by playing with light, shade and

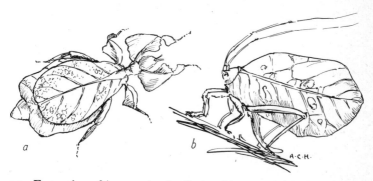

20. Examples of insects in the form of leaves: *a*, the leaf-insect *Phyllium crurifolium* and *b*, the grasshopper *Cycloptera excellens* (which actually reproduces the blotched appearance of a fungus infected leaf). See also the leaf-butterfly in fig. 28a (p. 130). From *The Living Stream*, p. 127.

123

tone values. It is to some of these artistic creations, and I use the words advisedly, that I want to draw your attention. We should note that the successful camouflage officers of the two world wars were artists rather than scientists, or sometimes scientists with artistic inclinations.

Any object appears solid to us very largely by the play of light and shade about its surfaces. In the outdoor daylight world illumination comes mainly from above. We can tell that an object is, say, a sphere, by the highlight on its top, which diminishes over its curved sides to pass with a gradually increasing shade into the deep black shadow of its underneath; but for this shading, we would not know whether the object was spherical or just a disc presented to us. If, as an artist, we wanted to destroy its appearance of solidity, we would paint it dark on the top and gradually merge this into paler shades of increasing lightness as we passed over the sides to a pure white on the underside as in fig. 21b. If we were good enough with our brush we should have made the object look quite flat (fig. 21c). It needed an artist who was also a naturalist, A. H. Thayer, to show us that this counter-shading principle, as he called it, was a general rule in animal coloration (fig. 22). Such a principle destroys the solid reality of the creature but if it were of one colour, however shaded, it

21. Illustrating Thayer's counter-shading principle. An object appears to have shape by the play of light and shade upon its surfaces; in normal outdoor illumination it has strong light above and shadow below as in *a*; a camouflage artist would counteract this effect by painting it dark on top, and grading the shading down the side to pure white below as in *b*; if well done this will destroy its appearance of solidity, as in *c*.

22. As Thayer first pointed out, the majority of animals living under normal conditions of daylight, unless protected by some other colour principle, tend to have a basic countershading coloration similar to *b* in fig. 21.

would still stand out against its background which is hardly ever uniform; nature, and I mean, of course, selection, again steps in and, again as if she were an artist, provides, in addition to the counter-shading, a colour pattern – a composition – which merges it into its surroundings (fig. 23).

It has sometimes been suggested that the counter-shading effect is a direct physiological one of greater pigment formation under the influence of light; while this may contribute to the effect in some cases, it is certainly not the whole explanation for often the pattern itself helps in the counter-shading effect. The black spots of the cheetah, for example, are more or less the same size, but are more crowded together on the back and then become progressively further apart down the

23. In a natural environment, of highlights and shadows, a counter-shaded animal with no other pattern would be more conspicuous than one with patches of light and dark upon it; such patterns are the general rule.
From *The Living Stream*, p. 128.

sides; whereas the shading of the guinea-fowl is seen to be produced by the little white spots which cover its grey plumage becoming larger as they approach the underside (fig. 24). There are interesting examples of animals which spend the daylight hours hanging upside down, such as the caterpillar of the eyed hawk-moth, and these are perfectly counter-shaded but in the opposite way to the normal; and there is the Nile catfish, which is similarly coloured and habitually swims belly upwards (fig. 25)!

Apart from its solid form the shape of an object may tell us what it is. In man's camouflage the disruptive colour principle is widely used on objects like tanks, lorries and guns, which are liable to be moved from one site to another. If blotched, with different colours, both light and dark, particularly at its edges, the general outline of an object is destroyed as it comes against the irregular patterns of light and shade of a typical landscape background. This is a principle widely developed in the animal kingdom. It is seen among mammals such as anteaters and many antelopes; many snakes have their surfaces broken up by light and dark 'designs' which tend to destroy their long cylindrical form against the foliage or dead leaves; and young birds and many moths provide excellent examples. The wings of moths,

24. The counter-shading effect may be produced by various means other than by simple shading; some particular pattern may be modified to give the same result, for example *a*, by black spots being closer together on the back than down the sides as in the cheetah, or *b*, by white spots on a dark ground being small on the back and getting larger and larger down the sides to the underneath as in the guinea-fowl (*Numida meleagris coronata*).

From *The Living Stream*, p. 130.

25. *a*, the caterpillar of the eyed hawk-moth (*Smerinthus ocellatus*) and *b*, the Nile catfish (*Synodontis batensoda*) are both counter-shaded in the reverse of the normal manner, having light backs and dark undersides. The former feeds at night and rests in the daytime hanging *upside down* as seen in the lower sketch; note how the dark lines along the oblique stripes now appear below them like the shadow of a raised rib on the underside of a leaf. This catfish habitually swims *upside down*. *a* is from a photograph and *b* (upper) redrawn from J. R. Norman: *A History of Fishes.*
From *The Living Stream*, p. 131.

which habitually rest during the day on exposed surfaces such as old walls and tree trunks, are instructive: note how the *edges* of the wings which would give away their shape are blotched, and so broken up, with contrasting light and dark pigment (fig. 26f). Particularly interesting is the 'use' of this disruptive principle in helping to hide that most conspicuous feature – the eye; again and again we see frogs, fish, ante-lopes and other animals, with a dark band of pigment cutting across the tell-tale eye and so reducing its emphasis as a focal point (see fig. 27).

More remarkable still are the types of coloration classed under the term of coincident disruptive patterns: bands and patches of colour on different parts of the body which are well separated from one another during active locomotion,

26. Examples of disruptive coloration: *a*, typical gun camouflage; *b*, South American anteater, note the typical 'gun camouflage' pattern on its long snout; *c*, young woodcock among woodland leaf litter; *d*, the Sargassum weed fish (*Pterophryne*); *e*, the eggs of the lapwing; and *f*, the garden carpet moth (*Xanthorhoë uctuata*) at rest on the lichen covered bark of an elm tree.
From *The Living Stream*, p. 132.

but come together, when an animal is at rest, to produce one complete 'design'. Such are frequently seen on the undersides of the wings of butterflies which, when at rest, with fore and hind wings together, present some particular camouflage pattern. Some examples of these are shown in fig. 28 including the veining of a leaf reproduced by the tropical leaf butterfly, the dead leaf effect of our own comma butterfly, and the beautiful green and white speckling on the underside of the hind wing of our orange-tip butterfly which at rest covers all but the tip of the fore wing (also green and white); in this last case the curved margin of the hind wing not only exactly fits and masks the bright orange patch, so conspicuous in flight, but merges the insect with the white and green of the cow-parsley flowers on which it so often rests. In the same figure I also include (*d*) the remarkable Central American butterfly *Thecla togarna*, whose coincident stripes

128

27. Examples of dark bands masking the eyes in a wide range of vertebrate animals: *a*, the common frog (*Rana temporaria*); *b*, the turnstone (*Strepsilus interpres*); *c*, the dotterel (*Endromias morinellus*); *d*, the gemsbok (*Oryx gazella*); *e*, the coral fish *Chæto-don*; and the South American boa (*Constrictor constrictor*). *a*, *d* and *f* are drawn from photographs by H. B. Cott in his *Adaptive Coloration in Animals*; *c* and *b* are redrawn from Hudson's *British Birds* and *e* from Portmann's *Animal Forms and Patterns*. From *The Living Stream*, p. 134.

suggest that the wings arise from the other end of the body where a false head, false eye and false antennae are represented to deflect the attacks of predators from the true head which is largely hidden between the front margins of the wings shown facing to the left. There are several species in this genus with *different* but *equally remarkable* coincident stripes accurately joining up across the fore and hind wings when at rest; *Thecla phaleros* with five instead of six such stripes is the one more usually figured.

Then there are often bands of colour across the limbs and backs of locusts which form one complete design. More exciting still are the series of bands of different colour and thickness to be found on the flanks of some species of frog; these are *reversed* in their order across the thighs, *reversed again* on the lower parts of the leg and *yet again* on the actual feet, so that when the frog is at rest, with its limbs folded up,

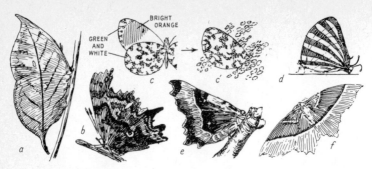

28. Examples of coincident disruptive coloration seen on the wings of butterflies and moths which, when at rest with their wings folded, present a continuous pattern carried on from one wing to the other to produce one complete 'design'. *a*, the leaf butterfly (*Kallima paralakta*); *b*, the comma butterfly (*Polygonia c-album*); *c*, *c'*, the orange-tip butterfly (*Euchlœ cardamines*); *d*, the butterfly *Thecla togarna* Hew (from Columbia); *e*, the purple thorn moth (*Selenia tetralunaria*) and *f*, the light barred moth (*Campœa margaritata*). All drawn from photographs except *d* which was drawn from a specimen in the Hope Department Collection at Oxford.
From *The Living Stream*, p. 136.

the bandings fit exactly together to present one whole design (fig. 29). It is just as if an artist had drawn his brush in single strokes of brown, yellow and green right across all four surfaces to distract from their normal anatomical form. It is a miracle of artistry; and incidentally it must be almost a miracle of gene action (under selection) to make the colour bands absolutely continuous when they come together. By this last sentence you may perhaps think I am trying to imply that I doubt whether such gene action can be the physical basis of these patterns. Just the opposite: I am sure that all the available evidence points to it and it is just this which makes one realize the *creative power* of selection.

These are surely works as creative as if they had been designed for the animals' concealment. Now here is the point I particularly want to make. All these wonderful effects – combining all the subtleties of the artist's craft as if with an

29. Further examples of coincident disruptive coloration: *a*, across the legs and wings of the grasshopper (*Œdipoda cœrulescens* and *b* and *c*, across the hind legs of the frogs *Edalorhina buckleyi* and *Bufo valliceps*. *b'* shows how the pattern in *b* will come together when the leg is in the resting position. *b* and *c* from photographs by Cott. From *The Living Stream*, p. 136.

understanding of the significance of light and shade, colour contrast, and tone values – could not possibly have been produced simply by the organisms themselves. They could not be produced, for instance, by any Lamarckian-like principle of the animal trying to make itself more like this or that; the colours and their effect are, of course, unseen by the animal itself. And moreover, they only become significant as camouflage when viewed at *some little distance* from the animal concerned. In other words, they could only be produced by the gradual selection of better and better imitations of natural objects or better and better optical illusions: *selection by some agent outside them*. This, as I have said, can only be by the action of predators which over long periods of evolutionary time have tended to miss those of their prey which happen to be coloured in such a fashion as to be a little less conspicuous than other members of their species. As the gene complex causes the animal to vary in this way and that, each time such a variation makes its possessor slightly less conspicuous, so will it stand a slightly better chance of surviving. This is why I have stressed this particular type of adaptation. It shows us all the effects – the tricks I might say – of the cunning creative artist; yet they can only have been produced by a form of selection. Whilst it *is* selection, it is well to remember at this point that these very subtle forms of adaptation are not those produced by a blind selection as by the inorganic environment, but a selection made by creatures, largely by vertebrate animals endowed with considerable powers of perception – yet actually by this perception being *deceived* by accidental resemblances. I shall return to the significance of this a little later.

Now this form of selection has not only 'created' subtleties of colour and form, but at the same time modified the actual behaviour of the animals concerned. We saw, earlier in the chapter, that the water-boatmen insects tended to settle on the backgrounds most nearly matching their own colour, and the same was true for the black and white varieties of the salt-and-pepper moth. Similar observations have also been made on the behaviour of different colour varieties of some birds.[7] We thus see many animals taking up special resting postures which will bring their camouflage pattern into the best relationship with the background upon which they are resting. Here, for example, in fig. 30, we see a hawk-moth

[7] Mayr in his *Systematics and the Origin of Species* (1942) writes on p. 86: 'Niethammer (1940) reviews the literature on cryptically colored larks, and his paper should be consulted for further details. In a series of colored plates, he illustrates the close correlation between soil and coloration of south-west African larks. The most remarkable part of this adaptation is that not only the general tone of color is reproduced accurately in the bird, but also its physical quality. The birds will have a smooth, even coloration, if they live on a fine-grained, dusty, or sandy soil. If, on the other hand, they live on a pebble desert, they will have a coarse disruptive pattern of coloration. Even more remarkable is the fact that the birds become very much attached to the soil to which they are adapted.' And on p. 247 he quotes Niethammer as follows: 'It is very striking in south-west Africa that reddish larks are found only on red soil, and dark ones on dark soil, even where two completely different types of soil meet . . .' He then goes on to describe how he tried to drive birds of one colour on to soil of another colour, but each time they at once flew back to their own colour backgrounds.

 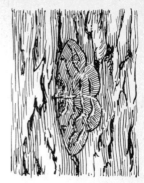

a *b*

30. Resting postures of moths on bark showing how instinctive behaviour acts with colour patterns to produce a camouflage effect. *a*, an East African hawk-moth (*Xanthopan m. morgani*) which rests with its head upwards, and *b*, the willow beauty moth (*Boarmia gammaria*) which rests with its body horizontal. Both drawn from photographs by Cott in his *Adaptive Coloration in Animals*. From *The Living Stream*, p. 138.

which has dark bands upon its wings that reproduce the shadows in the vertical cracks of the bark of a tree; it invariably rests with its head pointing upwards so that the bands reproduce the background. Other kinds, such as some of the geometrid moths, have bandings on their wings going *across from right to left* instead of down from front to back, and these, when at rest, settle with their body *horizontally* (also fig. 30) again bringing the wing pattern into line with the vertical bands on the bark, as beautifully illustrated by the observations and experiments of J. J. S. Cornes.[8] We see many other more elaborate behaviour patterns, particularly among some of the insects which mimic others and which I shall be discussing in a moment; for instance spiders, which mimic ants both in body shape and colour, run with their front pair of legs lifted up in an exact imitation of the ant's antennae.

[8] See J. J. S. Cornes, Attitude and Concealing Coloration, *Nature*, vol. 140, p. 684 (1937).

In all these examples it is certain that the creative element must be outside the organism, continually perfecting the chance patterns that happen to present a camouflage effect, or the chance idiosyncrasies in behaviour which just happen to enhance some particular illusion. I expect most of us at one time or another have looked upon the irregular patterns of the little marble chips let into the tessellated floor of a bathroom and seen among them some groupings that make us say to ourselves, 'That's a lizard,' or 'There's a man on horseback,' or 'a bird in flight' – some outline which at once reminds us of some more or less familiar object. Such chance variations in pattern must be continually occurring by random mutation and recombinations of different genes; whenever these make its possessor look, say, a little more like a leaf, perhaps by stripes which suggest its veins, then such will have a slight selective advantage and tend to escape destruction a little more often than others; such a pattern will gradually spread in the population. A little later perhaps, in another hundred years, another random change will make these striped forms which are now predominant in the population just a little further like a leaf and so the process goes on through aeons of time towards perfection. Some beautiful experimental studies on the reaction of predator birds to camouflaged caterpillars have been made by Dr L. de Ruiter[9] working under Dr Tinbergen at Oxford.

Whilst the camouflage or cryptic coloration provides us with such clear examples of a creative element in natural selection, the more specialized phenomena of 'mimicry' show us even greater refinements, but space will only allow me to touch on them. The term 'mimicry', I should explain for those who are not biologists, has for us a special limited meaning; it implies that one animal is 'mimicking' another animal, but we must think of the word 'mimicking' in quotes, because what we really mean is that the evolutionary

[9] Some experiments in the camouflage of stick caterpillars. *Behaviour*, vol. 4, pp. 222–32 (1952). Also, Countershading in caterpillars. *Archives Néerlandises de Zoologie*, vol. II (1955).

process has produced in one animal an imitation of another without any conscious act of mimicking. Now to explain mimicry I must discuss for a moment that other type of adaptive coloration given the name of 'warning' (or aposematic) coloration. Warning colours are just the opposite of camouflage; they are in fact advertising colours.

Nature uses advertisement to a remarkable extent. All the wonderful bright colours and shapes of flowers are attractive designs, like those on our café or inn signs, saying to the insects, 'Here be nectar – come and drink' – they 'pay' for their nectar, of course, by pollenating the flowers. The bright reds and orange colours of so many fruits and berries are again restaurant advertisements calling birds to come and dine, and in so doing unwittingly distribute the seeds of the plant.

The principle of warning coloration, first put forward by Wallace (p. 65), is based upon the association of some striking design with some noxious quality, such as the possession of a sting, an unpleasant odour or some poison which has been evolved for the protection of the animal concerned. Once such a quality has begun to develop by selection, in that the possessor tends to be left alone by predatory animals, then the advantage of advertisement at once becomes manifest. If any animal, having developed such a noxious quality, should also by chance mutation become coloured red or orange, it will tend to be left alone more than would otherwise be the case; would-be predators will learn to associate such a striking colour with the unpleasant consequence of the sting or other disagreeable character. A proportion of the population will be destroyed in the process of educating the predators, but the majority of the race will benefit.

Now to return to mimicry, I have said it is the copy of one animal by another and the essence of the matter is usually that of some quite *palatable* creature gaining protection by displaying the warning colours of another noxious species, thereby tending to be avoided by the predators that have learnt to leave such brightly coloured prey alone. This subterfuge, of course, has again been brought about, not by the intentional deceit of the mimic, but by the action of selection. In this country we see a wide variety of harmless insects, such as two-winged flies, some beetles and moths, all mimicking stinging bees and wasps. In the tropics we have remarkable examples among butterflies with some palatable species mimicking the elaborate and brilliant colour patterns of the noxious forms; the palatable mimicker, of course, must always be in the minority for the principle to work.[10] Some examples are given in figs. 31 and 32.

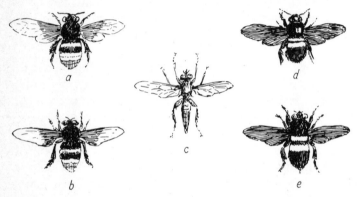

31. Bees mimicked by Asilid flies. *a*, the South American bee *Euglossa fasciata* mimicked by *b*, the fly *Mallophora fasciipennis*; *c*, an Asilid fly of typical form, *Andrenosoma vidua*; *d*, the African bee *Xylocopa inconstans* mimicked by *e*, the fly *Hyperechia bifasciata*. Drawn from specimens in the Hope Department collection at Oxford.

In addition to camouflage and warning colours I should just mention a third type of adaptive coloration with which we have not here been concerned: the colours of courtship display. Many birds and fish, and sometimes butterflies, often in the male sex only, display brilliant colours with

[10] There is a second kind of mimicry where two or more noxious species have the same colouring, sharing the same advertisement as it were.

which to coax their mates into submission to the sexual act or to advertise to rival males their possession of territory.

As a final point, which I shall only briefly mention here because it does not really affect my present argument concerning the reality of the power of selection and the range of genetic variability, I would point out a difference between the kind of selective action producing camouflage and that producing mimicry. Camouflage is the result of predators *failing* to perceive the cryptically coloured forms; the mimics on the other hand are not imitating natural objects in the usual sense, like leaves or twigs, but are 'copying' what are

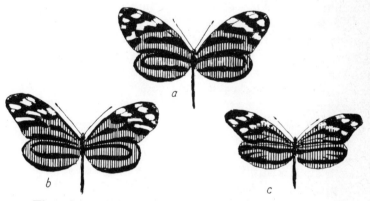

32. Three South American mimetic butterflies each belonging to a quite distinct family: *a*, *Melinæa imitata* (Ithomiinæ); *b*, *Heliconius telchinia* (Heliconiinæ) and *c*, *Dismorphia praxinoe* (Pieridæ). They each have the same colours: black, white and brilliant orange (shown shaded). *a* and *b* are Müllerian mimics and *c* a Batesian one. From *The Living Stream*, pp. 143 and 145.

much more like the designs of the abstract artist, brilliant colour patterns of arresting beauty, which have been evolved by the action of the predators themselves, i.e. selecting such 'designs' as aids to *their* 'memory': striking devices (like warning signals) to enable them to perceive the presence of danger (noxious taste or sting, etc.) before it is too late. I put the word memory, you will note, in quotes; whatever our views are about memory, however, we must recognize that the evolution of the mimics implies a constant *matching* of remarkably detailed patterns by the *perceiving* predators: the 'careful' comparison of one design with another which they have *previously* seen and, from their experience, *learnt* to avoid. It can only be this matching with an extraordinarily exact 'visual-memory' image which could produce the 'photographic' mimetic copies we are dealing with. I think it possible that here may be something of significance in biological philosophy that deserves greater attention.

I have chosen to consider adaptive coloration in this chapter because it seems to me to illustrate better than any other form of adaptation these three important points: (1) the almost infinite range of genetic variability that must be available to make possible the photographic-like copies of all manner of patterns and objects; (2) the creative power of the selection that carves out these copies from this mutable, genetic material; and (3) the fact that it is certain that all these elaborate adaptations, involving colour, pattern, shape *and behaviour*, and having every appearance of design, could only be the product of some external selective agent and *not* that of any Lamarckian-like mechanism. Whilst we see that the creative element in the forms of selection, which we have just been discussing, is the work of perceiving predators, this does not mean that an entirely 'blind' selection cannot also be creative; some of the adaptations of seeds for wind dispersal, embodying striking aerodynamic principles, are, as I have shown (see p. 70), just as much creative 'inventions', but produced entirely by the physical forces of the environment.

I must now warn you that I have, in part, been playing Devil's advocate. In addition to demonstrating their creative powers, the examples I have given of selection made by perceptive animals may give us cause for reflection about other possibilities in the mechanism. I believe all that I have said is true, but it is not the whole truth; there are other *selective* forces, equally important, but of quite a different kind, which we shall meet in our next chapter.

7

Organic and Behavioural Selection

The idea of organic selection was put forward quite independently at the end of the last century by three eminent
biologists: Mark Baldwin and Fairfield Osborn in America
and Lloyd Morgan in Great Britain – and then almost forgotten until quite recently. I have long regarded it as vital for
a better understanding of the Darwinian process. In the
introductory chapter (p. 18) I related how, in my address to
the zoology section of the British Association in 1949, I
expressed my view that 'A still more important contribution
that field zoology can make to evolutionary theory is to throw
more light on the part played by organic selection'; today if
what I am calling behavioural selection can be regarded as a
part of organic selection (as I then thought it was) I would
certainly say it is the *most* important contribution we can
make. Since then many people tell me that what I am calling
behavioural selection is a principle of a different kind; be that
as it may, the purpose of this chapter is to explain just why I
regard this behavioural selection as of such significance.

Here is another remarkable example, like that of Darwin
and Wallace and the idea of natural selection, of different
naturalists at the same time putting forward an entirely new,
but similar concept. I have said it was almost forgotten for
many years; it might have been better if I had said it was
lightly dismissed as the 'Baldwin Effect' with the implication
that it was something of only minor importance. G. G.
Simpson has a valuable general review article on the subject

139

in the journal *Evolution*, Vol. 7 (1952) and here puts his finger on the reason for the neglect of these ideas; they were put forward, he says, 'shortly before the rediscovery of Mendelism gave a radically different turn to biological thought'.

I have dealt very fully with the origin of the theory of organic selection in Chapter 6 of *The Living Stream* with all the references to the different publications; here I will briefly summarize the course of events. Lloyd Morgan gave a lecture on his views to the New York Academy of Sciences on 31 January 1896 and immediately, in the discussion which followed, both Baldwin and Osborn expressed very similar ideas; in the same year all three published papers on the subject in the American journals *Science*, *American Naturalist*, or *The Transactions of the New York Academy of Science* – a most interesting series to refer back to. Then in April 1897 Baldwin, in consultation with Morgan and Osborn, published a summary of their views in *Nature*. This is too long to quote here, and being written three years before the rediscovery of Mendel's laws it is phrased in terms which, for the modern reader, are not very easy to follow; instead I am going to quote two passages from Sir Julian Huxley's *Evolution, the Modern Synthesis*. These two statements are particularly useful because they illustrate two different aspects of organic selection.

In the first example Huxley (his p. 304) discusses the remarkable experiments of Dr W. H. Thorpe[1] demonstrating the establishment of an olfactory conditioning in insects in relation to their particular sources of food; parasitic ichneumon flies conditioned to the chemical nature of their hosts or the fruit fly *Drosophila* conditioned to lay its eggs in a peppermint scented medium after having been reared in such an essence during early larval life. He writes as follows:

[1] *Proc. Roy. Soc.* Series B, vol. 124 (1937), p. 56; vol. 126 (1938), p. 370; vol. 127 (1939), p. 424.

We have here a beautiful special case of the principle of organic selection, as enunciated by Baldwin and Lloyd Morgan, according to which modifications repeated for a number of generations may serve as the first step in evolutionary change, not by becoming impressed upon the germ-plasm, but by holding the strain in an environment where mutations tending in the same direction will be selected and incorporated into the constitution. The process simulates Lamarckism but actually consists in the replacement of modifications by mutations.

For those who are biologists I should like to say that I believe this aspect of organic selection is the same as that called genetic assimilation by the late Professor C. H. Waddington who carried out a series of beautiful experiments to demonstrate it. I have discussed the similarity of the two principles in *The Living Stream* (pp. 167–9).

Huxley's second important reference to organic selection in his *Evolution, the Modern Synthesis* (pp. 523–4) is where he describes it as a principle 'according to which an organism may in the first instance become adapted to an ecological niche merely by behaviour (whether genetic or purely habitual) and any consequent non-heritable modifications, after which mutations for the kind of structural change suitable to the particular mode of life will have a better chance of being selected. Where the modifications are extensive, the process of their replacements by mutations may closely simulate Lamarckism. The principle is an important one which would appear to have been unduly neglected by recent evolutionists.'

Now Huxley does refer here to *structural change*. Let me repeat the significant sentence:

. . . after which mutations for the kind of structural change suitable to the particular mode of life will have a better chance of being selected.

That is the essence of my thesis; only I would say, as I am sure Huxley also means, not only by mutation but also by re-assortment and combination of existing genes. I am saying nothing original. But what I am doing, which I believe *is* new, is to say, jointly with Dr R. F. Ewer whose views I shall discuss presently, that this is not just a slight subsidiary effect, but is one of the major factors in the evolutionary process; the changing habits of animals, at any rate in the higher vertebrates, the birds and mammals, is indeed a powerful agent within the Darwinian system.

No one will deny that animals living under natural conditions may come to change their behaviour; such new habits may no doubt often be due to alterations in their environment, such as failure of food supplies or the destruction of breeding sites and so on, but sometimes they may be formed through the animals themselves discovering new ways of life. They are, as I have said, inquisitive, exploratory creatures. Among the higher vertebrates a new piece of behaviour, perhaps, for example, in the gathering of food, if adopted by one or two individuals and then seen by others to be advantageous, will gradually spread by copying through the community and be passed on from parent to offspring. We see, in fact, in birds and mammals, the beginning of what might be called a tradition. In any population of animals among which there has come about a change of habit, there will turn up sooner or later individuals having small variations in structure which will make them more efficient in relation to their new behaviour; over a period of time these kinds will tend to survive rather better than those less well-equipped in this particular respect, and so the composition of the population will gradually change.

As an illustration let me use an imaginary example that I have used before:[2] that of birds which mainly lived by picking off insects from the surface of tree-trunks. If, perhaps in some period of shortage, one or two more enterprising individuals started probing with their beaks into

[2] *Proc. Linn. Soc. Lond.*, vol. 168 (1957), pp. 85–7.

cracks in the bark and found that they could get more insects by doing so, and then developed this new habit, they might be copied by others of the same species, and so gradually we would see a change of behaviour spreading through the populations. This is not just supposition. Our common bird, the great tit (*Parus major*), took to opening the tops of milk-bottles left by the milkmen on their customers' door-steps, and so getting at the rich cream at the top; this new behaviour spread rapidly across the country, apparently by copying, and extended right through populations of Europe.[3] At first the milk-bottle tops were cardboard lids; later, however, in an attempt to defeat the tits, the dairies introduced the metal caps. Were the tits beaten? Not a bit of it. Here, indeed, we see the result of enterprising exploratory behaviour spreading throughout the range of the species where milk-bottles are available. Soon the great tits were being copied by another species, the smaller blue tit (*Parus caeruleus*).

Then there is the new habit developed by the greenfinch (*Ligurinus chloris*) which recently took to attacking the seeds of the shrub, *Daphne*; beginning in the north of England, this new behaviour has since been seen to spread southwards county by county, again presumably by being copied and passed on.[4] A more remarkable example is the behaviour observed by Jane Goodall and her husband Hugo van Lawick who saw and photographed Egyptian vultures picking up stones in their beaks and then hurling them with such force at ostrich eggs that they broke the shell and allowed the vultures to eat the contents. This proved not to be just an isolated instance, for they set out two ostrich eggs at a site some sixty miles away and waited to see what would happen; sure enough, before long, a pair of these vultures appeared and performed the same, almost tool-using, act.[5] This must surely be a new habit developed in the first place by some

[3] R. A. Hinde and J. Fisher, *British Birds*, vol. 44 (1952), pp. 393–6.
[4] Max Petterson, *Nature*, vol. 134 (1959), p. 649.
[5] *Nature*, vol. 212 (1966), pp. 1468–9.

more enterprising individuals. I have myself watched the large Dominican gulls (*Larus dominicanus*) stealing eggs from the colony of jackass penguins on Dassen Island off the coast of South Africa and carrying them in their widely-opened beaks to drop them upon a flat rock from a height of some forty feet; they then swoop down to feed on the yolk or developing young.[6] Or again, there is the Californian sea-otter which habitually feeds by using a stone to break open sea-urchins and various forms of shell-fish, to say nothing of the well-known practice of the thrush breaking its snails on an 'anvil' stone.

The beautiful studies by Drs Itani and Kawai of the social life of wild monkeys in Japan show the copying of new behaviour-patterns such as potato-washing spreading through the colony and being transmitted from one generation to another.[7] Recently Professor Tinbergen has drawn attention to two different methods of opening mussel-shells employed by those wading birds, the oyster-catchers; these are not genetically determined but represent two separate traditions of feeding which are passed on by parent to offspring.[8]

After this digression to contemporary examples showing that the development of new behaviour-patterns and their spread are very much a reality, I will now return to my original hypothetical example of birds probing into the bark of trees for insects. If this new habit became well established in the species and, being more profitable, replaced the old practice of pecking insects off the surface, then any members of the population with a gene-complex providing a beak slightly better-adapted to such probing would have a better chance of survival than those less well-equipped. A new shape of beak would be evolved as a result of a change of

[6] *Great Waters* (Collins, London, 1967), p. 248.
[7] J. Itani in *Primates*, vol. I (Inuyama, 1958), pp. 84–98, and M. Kawai, ibid., vol. 6 (1964), pp. 1–30.
[8] The Croonian Lecture for 1972, *Proceedings of the Royal Society*, Series B, vol. 182 (1972), pp. 395–6.

habit. When I first discussed this I had thought, as I said at the time, that I was merely recalling the views which had been put forward by Mark Baldwin and Lloyd Morgan at the turn of the century. Now, some people tell me that I am reading too much into Baldwin's views and that what I am saying is really something different. Most people, however, when I discuss it, tell me I am simply talking pure Darwinism and that I am just making a fuss about nothing. This is where I disagree and insist that there is a real, if subtle, difference which is fundamental to our understanding of the evolution process. I shall try to explain why.

Because the change of habit is often occasioned by changes in the environment, it is generally supposed, I think, that any selection due to such a change of habit is one differing only in degree, but not in kind, from other forms of Darwinian selection. This for me is the crux of the whole issue; I think they are radically different. I realize, of course, that it is the differential mortality in the population which brings about the survival of the more efficient type of beak in our example, and that this is obviously mediated by various factors in the environment killing off a higher proportion of the less efficient forms; nevertheless the real *initiating agent* in the process is the new behaviour-pattern, the *new habit*. I believe the case for regarding this 'behavioural' type of selection as different in kind from other forms of natural selection can be maintained. Although new habits may, as I have said, frequently result from environmental changes, they are by no means always so formed; among vertebrates it must often be the restless, exploring and perceptive animals that discover new ways of living, new sources of food, just as the tits discovered the food value of opening the tops of milk bottles or the vultures took to breaking ostrich eggs. This searching, inquisitive type of behaviour has no doubt been fostered and developed by selection just because it pays dividends.

Let me now come back to a consideration of the beaks of birds which I took as my first example of the way behavioural selection might work. Here I will quote from the late Dr

David Lack's beautiful study of *Darwin's Finches* which I have already referred to on p. 59. In his chapter 6 (p. 55) he makes a special study of the beak differences of these finches in relation to their food. He writes as follows:

> The chief way in which the various species of Darwin's finches differ from each other is in their beaks. Indeed, the beak differences are so pronounced that systematists have at various times used as many as seven different generic names for the birds. In this book the genera are reduced to four, but it is convenient to retain the other generic names as subgenera, since they emphasize the adaptive radiation of the finches. . . .

He then goes on to give details of the feeding habits of the different sub-genera in relation to shapes of beak, and ends as follows:

> To summarize, the beak differences between most of the genera and sub-genera of Darwin's finches are clearly correlated with differences in feeding methods. This is well borne out by the heavy, finch-like beak of the seed-eating *Geospiza*, the long beak of the flower-probing *Cactornis*, the somewhat parrot-like beak of the leaf-, bud- and fruit-eating *Platyspiza*, the woodpecker-like beak of the woodboring *Cactospiza*, and the warbler-like beaks of the insect-eating *Certhidea* and *Pinaroloxias*. Only in one group, namely the insectivorous tree-finches of the sub-genera *Camarhynchus* (*sens. strict.*) is the beak not particularly suggestive of the feeding habits; these birds, though feeding primarily on insects, may be regarded as moderately unspecialized in both diet and beak.

The differences in the beaks are illustrated in fig. 33.

Which is the more reasonable explanation of these adaptations: that chance mutations, first occurring in a few members of the population, caused these birds to alter their habits and seek new food supplies more suitable to their beaks and

33. Beak differences in Darwin's finches on the central islands of Galapagos, all ⅔ natural size redrawn from Lack (after Swarth): *top row*, the genus *Geospiza*, *a*, *G. magnirostris*; *b*, *G. fortis*; *c*, *G. fuliginosa*; *d*, *G. difficilis debilirostris*; *e*, *G. scandeus*; *middle row*, the genus *Camarhynchus*, *f*, *C. crassirostris*; *g*, *C. psittacula*; *h*, *C. pavulus*; *i*, *C. pallidus*; *j*, *C. heliobates*; *bottom row*, *k*, *Certhidea olivacæ*, and *l*, *Pinaroloxias inornata*.
From *The Living Stream*, p. 175.

so become a more successful and surviving race, or did the birds, forced by competition, adopt new feeding habits which spread in the population so that chance changes in beak form giving greater efficiency came gradually to be preserved by organic selection?

Differences of habit clearly play a great part in the ways of life of these different species. Can we really doubt which of the two explanations just suggested is the more likely to be true? It is among these finches that we meet with one of the most remarkable examples of the exploring perceptive behaviour of animals. I quote again from Lack, from the same chapter:

The woodpecker-finch *Camarhynchus pallidus* has a stout, straight beak, with obvious affinities to that of the

147

insectivorous tree-finches, but more elongated, and modified in the direction of that of a woodpecker or nuthatch. It feeds on beetles and similar insects, for which it searches bark and leaf clusters, and less commonly the ground, and also bores into wood. It is much more exclusively insectivorous than the insectivorous tree-finches, and with this can be correlated the greater specialization of its beak. *C. pallidus* further resembles a woodpecker in that it climbs up and down vertical trunks and branches. It is the only one of Darwin's finches to do this. It also possesses a remarkable, indeed a unique, habit.[9] When a woodpecker has excavated in a branch for an insect, it inserts its long tongue into the crack to get the insect out. *C. pallidus* lacks the long tongue, but achieves the same result in a different way. Having excavated, it picks up a cactus spine or twig, one or two inches long, and holding it lengthwise in its beak, pokes it up the crack, dropping the twig to seize the insect as it emerges. In the arid zone the bird uses one of the rigid spines of the prickly pear *Opuntia*, but in the humid zone, where there is no *Opuntia*, it breaks off a small twig of suitable length from a tree or bush. It has been seen to reject a twig if it proved too short or too pliable. Sometimes the bird carries a spine or twig about with it, poking it into cracks and crannies as it searches one tree after another. This remarkable habit, first reported by Gifford (1919) and fully confirmed first by W. H. Thompson and later by the writer, is one of the few recorded uses of tools in birds. The nearest parallel is the use of fruits by the bower-bird *Ptilonorhynchus violaceus* for staining the stems of its bower.

To return to the structural diffences in these finches in general, let me quote again from Dr Lack (*loc. cit.*, p. 148):

[9] Since this was written another member of the same genus, *C. heliobates*, has been shown by E. Curio and P. Kramer (*Z. Tierpsychol.*, vol, 21, pp. 223–34, 1964) to have a similar habit.

I consider that adaptive radiation of Darwin's finches can have come about only through the repeated differentiation of geographical forms, which later met and became established in the same region, that this in turn led to subdivision of the food supply and habitats, and then to an increased restriction in ecology and specialization in structure of each form. On Cocos, where conditions are unsuitable for species-formation, there has likewise been no adaptive radiation among the land birds.

Such subdivision of the food supply and habits clearly implies the development of different behaviour patterns.

Now in fig. 34 let us look at the diversity of beaks among birds in general. Can it really be maintained that it is *more likely* that random mutations forced these different groups of birds to their different modes of life, rather than that they developed different habits and that such differences in feeding led gradually to beaks better and better adapted to their

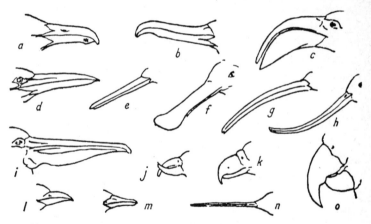

34. A selection of beaks of birds of various habits: *a*, herring gull; *b*, frigate bird; *c*, flamingo; *d*, gannet; *e*, snipe; *f*, spoonbill; *g*, curlew; *h*, avocet; *i*, pelican; *j*, cross-bill; *k*, eagle; *l*, swallow; *m*, spotted flycatcher; *n*, humming-bird; *o*, parrot.
From *The Living Stream*, p. 177.

ways of life? Surely it must be admitted that it is change of habit which is the dominating factor influencing such selection. Now if we had been looking at a chart showing not the forms of beaks but the legs and feet of these birds would we not have come to a similar conclusion?

I believe the same principle will apply to the evolution of all the higher vertebrate animals and particularly the mammals, which have developed so many new ways of life such as digging in the ground or climbing trees for food, diving into water after fish – indeed some becoming entirely aquatic as the whales – or flying like the bats. Does a terrestrial animal by chance get webbed feet and then take to the water to use them? Of course not. We can imagine the ancestors of the otter, before they took to swimming, watching fish in shallow water, and one, more enterprising than the rest, diving in and catching a fish, repeating the process and so developing this new way of hunting. It would be copied by others farther up the stream so that before long this new habit of aquatic feeding might spread through the population. Even now the young have to be taught to swim by their parents. Once it became a well-established way of life, new chance mutations giving webbing to the feet would make swimming more successful, so that those possessing this advantage would tend to survive better than others. This would be a change brought about *within* the Darwinian system – but one originating in a change of behaviour, through the animal's inquisitive exploratory activity. All the major adaptations which distinguish the main diverging lines of animal evolution are essentially, I believe, examples of what I would call *behavioural selection*.

A number of other biologists have independently been coming to similar conclusions. Dr R. F. Ewer[10] emphasizes the same effect, saying that 'behaviour will tend to be always one jump ahead of structure, and so play a decisive role in the

[10] *New Biology*, vol. 13 (Penguin, London, 1952), pp. 117–19, and *Acta Biotheoretica*, vol. 13 (Leiden, 1960, pp. 161–84).

evolutionary process'. Professor C. H. Waddington points out that 'an animal by its behaviour contributes in a most important way to determining the nature and intensity of the selection pressures which will be exerted on it'.[11] Ernst Mayr, one of the greatest American authorities on evolution, has been coming to similar views, and in 1970 sums up his conclusions thus: 'Changes in behaviour, such as a preference for a new habitat, food, or mode of locomotion, may set up new selection pressures. Much evidence indicates that most major evolutionary shifts (the origin of higher taxa) began with a behavioural shift.'[12] In the same year even Jacques Monod, in his *Le hasard et la nécessité*, was saying the same thing; I quote from p. 121 of the English translation, *Chance and Necessity* (1972): 'It is also evident that the initial choice of this or that kind of behaviour can often have very long range consequences, not only for the species in which it first appears in rudimentary form, but for all its descendants, even if they constitute an entire evolutionary subgroup.'

Whilst, as I have already said, a great deal of animal evolution must be produced, like the evolution of plants, by the selective action of the environment, I believe that what I am calling behavioural selection may be something much more fundamental to the whole evolution and philosophy of life. It is the behavioural side of animal life which has fashioned the form of the body from the material world by the continual selection within a population of those chance genetic varieties which give the better manifestation of its pattern of activity. The death of the body is an absolute necessity in a progressive evolution of better and better incarnations of a gradually changing behavioural element – the 'spirit of life' if you like. The organs, the parts of the body, the hands and feet and so on, are all tools carved out of the physical world by the behavioural selection I have dis-

[11] *Nature*, vol. 183 (1959), pp. 1134–8.
[12] Verhandlungen der Deutschen Zoologischen Gesselschaft, vol. 64 (1970), pp. 322–36.

cussed. It is, I believe, the mental element in the universe that is the real operating factor in animal evolution; the constantly varying DNA code supplies the changing material for this selection to work on.

To what extent are these changes in behaviour conscious ones? This is the question we must ask in the next chapter; certainly not all of them, for we have seen innate behaviour patterns developed to accompany camouflage colouring of which the animal itself cannot be aware.

8

Consciousness the Key

We are now reaching the turning point in our consideration of Darwinian evolution and its relationship to what we may call the spiritual nature of man.

I hope that my argument up to here will have convinced you, if you were not already so convinced, of the reality not only of the evolutionary process but of the part Darwinian selection plays within it. I hope also that the evidence presented in the last chapter will have shown that the factors governing selection need not be entirely the product of events in an animal's surroundings, either physical or animate (i.e. predators or competitors), but may be brought about by changes in the behaviour of the animal itself. We have further seen that whilst these behavioural changes may often be brought about through changes in the environment, this is by no means always so; perhaps just as often they may be caused by the animal's inquisitive, exploratory nature discovering new ways of life.

Now suppose animals are conscious beings? And here I do not necessarily mean self-conscious beings like grown humans (this we may never know, although see later, p. 162); but I mean at least as conscious as little children before they fully grasp their individuality. Up to now there has been a taboo that has prevented biologists from considering animal behaviour as a conscious activity; this has been natural because it has not yet been possible in scientific terms to relate consciousness to what we know of the physico-chemical mechanism of the animal body.

Here I would like to emphasize a distinction to which I

have often drawn attention before: the difference between natural history and science. The former, as the word history implies, is the qualitative, observational description of the natural world, whereas science is the quantitative study of nature by means of measurement and experiment. Much of biology has been derived from descriptive natural history which has paved the way for a later truly scientific treatment, as we see in quantitative ecology or ethology (the experimental study of animal behaviour in the wild). I like, nevertheless, to point out that the greatest contribution that biology has yet made to our philosophy came originally not from the biological laboratories, but from the observations of the great field naturalists of the last century: Darwin, Wallace, Bates and so many more. Evolution did not become strictly a part of quantitative science until the finding of Mendel's laws – nearly twenty years after Darwin's death – led to the statistical studies of genetics, and then much later the molecular biological discoveries of the genetic code gave a new scientific dimension to a part of the process. Much of our understanding of evolution, however, is still in the realm of observational natural history.

Now, in the latter part of our book, we shall see the naturalists of human experience providing the evidence for a part of the living system which can no longer be intellectually ignored: an overwhelming demonstration, I believe, of a part of man's natural history that can only be described in spiritual terms. Why am I not waiting until I have presented this evidence before mentioning it as part of our discussion? It is because, if I am right in my assessment of this evidence, it must make a radical difference to the way we look at Darwinian theory. There are two courses open to us. Either we wait until the end of the book when we have considered the evidence for this spirituality and then come back to look again at evolution, or I make passing reference to it here whilst what we have been saying about the theory is fresh in our minds. I choose the latter course, but only mention it because I feel sure it must belong to the same part of nature as does consciousness.

As I have said often before, science cannot deal with the real essence of religious feeling any more than it can touch the nature of art, or our joy in the glories of natural beauty or the poetry of human love. Many scientists have dismissed (quite irrationally, I believe) religious feelings as only superstition or childish wishful thinking, but surely no intellectual will deny the reality of our love of art, music, natural beauty or of adventure. Our appreciation of all these lie in our field of consciousness; whilst not strictly amenable to quantitative science the records of spiritual experience can be examined systematically by the naturalists of human nature. Biologists cannot have it both ways; if we are one with the animal kingdom, as they all must believe, consciousness, not necessarily self-consciousness, must be an essential part of the living system. Can we conceive of such a fundamental aspect of life being confined to one species of animal – man?

Can anyone who has kept and become fond of a dog, a cat or a horse believe that they are unconscious organic machines? Can we read such accounts as Mrs Joy Adamson's friendship with her lioness in her book *Born Free* (1960), or of Gavin Maxwell's affectionate otters in his *Ring of Bright Water* (1960), or again of Miss Len Howard's studies of *Birds as Individuals* (1952), and be in any doubt that there is as much, or almost as much, ground for regarding such animals as conscious beings as we have for attributing this quality to little children? Lacking the reasoned thought and intelligence of ourselves, they will, of course, have nothing like the same conception of their surroundings as we have through our education and tradition.

The ethologist, Dr John H. Crook, in his book *The Evolution of Human Consciousness* (Clarendon Press, Oxford, 1980), has the following most interesting passage (his p. 242) regarding the difference in consciousness between animals and man:

155

I am arguing that the most crucial evolutionary emergent in the phylogeny of human powers is the ability whereby the person conceives of himself as an active agent distinguishable as an entity from others and about which propositions can be entertained. It is of course this capacity that gives depth and meaning to human transactions and allows of their development within a given culture. We know remarkably little about the evolutionary origins of the capacity to represent oneself to oneself as a self. Even advanced mammals interact with one another on a level of awareness that appears to lack this component, which evidently requires a cognitive apparatus present only in man and perhaps to a degree in the great apes. In an experiment with captive animals, Gallup (1970) provided rhesus monkeys and chimpanzees with mirrors in which they could observe their reflected images. Within each species two groups were anaesthetized and one of the groups received dabs of dye on cheek and ear while the control group did not. On awakening the animals observed their faces in mirrors. Chimpanzees used their reflections to touch their *own* noses, thus demonstrating an awareness that the image represented themselves and showed a change in their appearance. The Rhesus monkeys failed to show this self-directed behaviour. Human infants can recognize themselves in this way at least by the age of fifteen months (Lewis and Brooke, 1977).

Another biologist who was prepared to acknowledge these difficult problems of consciousness was the late Professor C. H. Waddington, in *The Ethical Animal* (1960, p. 63); here he says that 'As soon as one places the problem of free will in juxta-position with that of consciousness, it becomes apparent that it cannot be solved either by manipulation of our existing physico-chemical concepts ... We need ideas which depart more radically from those of the physical sciences ...'

I was delighted that that great scientist, the late Sir Cyril Hinshelwood, gave such prominence to the question of consciousness in his last presidential address to the Royal Society, that of 1959.[1]

> It is surprising [he said] that biological discussions often under-estimate human consciousness as a fundamental experimental datum. In science we attach no value to unverifiable deductions, or to empty qualitative statements, but nobody defends the neglect of experimental data. Among these we cannot validly disregard those of our own consciousness except by a deliberate abstraction for which we must assume responsibility, and which we should not forget having made . . .

He then proceeds to show that we are in fact all the time trying experiments – not, of course, in a laboratory sense but nevertheless experiments – in our relations with other people by informing, asking, ordering, obeying, resisting and so on with various emotions and observing the results. The hypothesis that other people have an inner life not unlike our own is tested again and again in the daily experiments we make with them; it enables us to register correspondences at point after point in so intimate a way that we accept the hypothesis, if not as absolute truth, then as something nearly as good. And then Hinshelwood says, 'with most of the basic conclusions of science I am in no position to demand more'. After more discussion of the problem he continues, 'There is at present no obvious answer to the question of what kind of advance can possibly be hoped for in the problem of psychophysical concomitance. This, however, is no reason for giving up thought which at least helps to avoid the kind of errors so easily made both about physics and about biology when the problem is ignored . . .'

I think it likely that we cannot hope to solve the problem if, as scientists, we continue to look at it only from the physicochemical side. And on logical grounds I can see no reason

[1] *Proceedings of the Royal Society*, Series A, vol. 253 (1959), pp. 439–49.

why we should draw a line at some arbitrary point in evolutionary time between the higher members of the primate stock, the ancestors of man, who are conscious beings, and those earlier 'more animal' members whom we might, in shallower thought, have imagined (as many people have apparently so imagined in the past) to be creatures lacking this sense of awareness.

It was equally good to hear what the present president of the Royal Society, Sir Andrew Huxley, said in his address to the Society in 1981 when he defended, as did his ancestor Thomas Henry, Darwinian evolution against the recent attacks being made upon it. He proclaimed that 'the biggest of all problems for biology – too often swept under the carpet – is the existence of consciousness, for which present-day physics and chemistry do not contain so much as the necessary dimension'.

I will return again for a moment to the views of Sir Cyril Hinshelwood as expressed in his presidential address to the British Association at Cambridge in 1965 entitled *Science and the Scientists*.[2] He spoke as follows:

> Some philosophers have wanted to talk away the mind-matter problem as a verbal confusion. I suspect that at bottom they simply attach no importance to the scientific description of things and are therefore indifferent to any divorce between it and the language which describes the world of conscious experience. If so they are of course entitled to remain indifferent, but men of science presumably do not.
>
> At all the boundaries of science we come against what are probably the inherent limitations of human understanding. At the edge of biology we meet the chasm between what science describes and what the mind experiences. In the physical sciences too we encounter insoluble contradictions if we try to contemplate the limits of space or the beginning of time . . . If reality is

[2] *The Advancement of Science*, vol. 22 (1965), pp. 347–56.

describable by a four-dimensional space-time continuum why does the time dimension present itself differently to our consciousness?

In the same address he discusses the work and views of the late Sir Charles Sherrington, saying:

> Though he more than any other man elucidated the nature of the nervous reflexes, he was strongly opposed to any mechanistic view of the world. 'Mind' he wrote, 'knows itself and knows the world: chemistry and physics, explaining so much, cannot undertake to explain mind itself.'

Sherrington, in a memorable passage in his Gifford Lectures *Man on His Nature* (p. 318) says:

> We have, it seems to me, to admit that energy and mind are phenomena of two categories . . . Mind as attaching to any unicellular life would seem to me to be unrecognizable to observation; but I would not feel that permits me to affirm it is not there. Indeed, I would think, that since mind appears in the developing soma[3] that amounts to showing that it is potential in the ovum (and sperm) from which the soma sprang.

The late Professor Michael Polanyi in his famous Gifford Lectures published as *Personal Knowledge* (1958) makes an important distinction by dividing knowledge into two main kinds and by so doing emphasizes that man's mental life is not only in one important and obvious respect radically different from that of his animal ancestry, but is in another more fundamental way much nearer to the animal world than perhaps has ever been thought before, even by the most confirmed evolutionists. His two kinds of knowledge are (1) *explicit knowledge*, that which is formulated in words, maps, mathematical symbols, etc., and (2) *tacit knowledge*, that

[3] For those who are not biologists I should explain that the term *soma* means the body as distinct from the reproductive germ cells.

which is not so formulated, for example the knowledge of what we are in the act of doing or experiencing before we express it in words or symbols. When we go for a country walk by ourselves we gain a knowledge of the scenery through which we are passing and we appreciate its beauty without necessarily describing it to ourselves in words; only later, on getting home, we may give a verbal description of it.

The more primitive forms of human knowing – those forms of intelligence which man shares with animals – are situated, says Polanyi, behind the barrier of language. Animals have no speech (beyond systems of communication by signs and sounds); the towering superiority of man over the animals is almost entirely due to his development of language. Speech enables man to formulate ideas, to reflect upon them, and communicate them to others. Babies up to eighteen months or so are said to be not much superior to chimpanzees of the same age; only when they learn to speak do they leave the apes far behind. Even adult humans, however, show no distinctly greater intelligence than animals, so long as their minds work unaided by language. 'In the absence of linguistic clues,' says Polanyi, 'man sees things, hears things, feels things, moves about, explores his surroundings and gets to know his way about very much as animals do.' Man, of course, with his tradition of explicit knowledge and the long extension of the period of his growing up, and so learning by speech-communication, has a vastly larger conscious conception of the nature of his environment than any animal could possibly have; nevertheless we have no right to assume that there has been a radical break in evolution with the sudden creation of conscious awareness at some point in early human history. It perhaps may not be far from the truth to think of the conscious awareness of the higher animals to be, as I have already suggested, somewhat like that of little children.

My bringing in Polanyi's views at this point may appear at first sight to be somewhat of a digression from our main argument. I discuss them because I believe that they do *conclusively* show that there is such a state of consciousness in at any rate the higher vertebrate animals: furthermore, such a demonstration of their conscious actions is, I believe, of the greatest importance for our appreciation of the part played by behaviour in the course of Darwinian evolution.

When my earlier book *The Living Stream* had already gone to press my attention was drawn to a book *The Method of Evolution* published in 1900 by Professor H. W. Conn and quoted in an appendix to Mark Baldwin's book *Development and Evolution* (1902). I realized at once that he held views very similar to my own and likewise derived them from those of Lloyd Morgan and Baldwin which I discussed in the last chapter; I therefore, when my book was in proof, added it as an addendum note at the end of my chapter on behaviour as a selective force. I had at first intended discussing it in the last chapter, but as he introduces consciousness I have felt it better to bring it in here. It should be noted that as he published it in 1900 it was clearly written, as were Baldwin's and Lloyd Morgan's theses, before Mendel's laws were known; nevertheless he writes of genetic changes in an almost modern way, calling them congenital variations. I will quote a brief extract:

Perhaps a concrete case may make this somewhat obscure theory a little clearer. Imagine, for example, that some change in conditions forced an early monkey-like animal, that lived on the ground, to escape from its enemies by climbing trees. [We now know that the primate stock came from earlier aboreal animals like the tree-shrews, but his argument on the original adaptations to a climbing life is valid.] This arboreal habit was so useful to him that he continued it during his life, and his offspring, being from birth kept in the trees, acquired the same habit. Now it would be sure to follow that the new method of using their muscles would soon adapt them more closely to the duty of climbing . . . All this would take place without any necessity for a congenital variation or the inheritance of any character which especially adapted the monkey for life in the trees.

'But, in the monkeys thus preserved, congenital variations would be ever appearing in all directions. It would be sure to follow that after a time there might be some congenital variation that affected the shape of the hands and feet. These would not be produced as the result of the use of the organs or as acquired variations, but simply from variations in the germ plasm.'

He then goes on to consider consciousness as a factor in evolution in exactly the same way as I have been doing here; these are exactly my views, written some fifty years before I was coming to them. I will now continue my quotation:

This conception of the action of selection evidently makes consciousness a factor in evolution. It has always been claimed by the Lamarckian school that consciousness aids in the process of descent. It has sometimes been supposed that by this claim is meant that by conscious efforts an animal can modify its structure; but such a conception has certainly not been held by scientists in recent years. Consciousness may, however, lead to the use of organs or to the adoption of the new habits, and, if the view we are now considering be sound, such use of organs, or such habits, leads to the development of acquired characters which enable the individual to live in new conditions more successfully, *until after a time congenital variations take their place.* Consciousness thus becomes an indirect factor in evolution. (my italics)

How far down the animal kingdom must we go before we reach a point at which consciousness may have arisen in the course of evolution? I cannot imagine a point at which so fundamental a feature of life suddenly appeared. I confess I follow the great scientific philosopher A. N. Whitehead in believing that it is to be found in the very lowest forms of life. I believe it is likely to be a very property of life itself. You will remember what Sherrington said (in my quotation on p. 159) regarding mind in unicellular organisms, that whilst it would seem to him to be unrecognizable to observation, that would not permit him to affirm that it was not there. Now let me refer to the views of the greatest student of the behaviour of the unicellular protozoan animals, Professor H. S. Jennings; he writes as follows in his classic volume *The Behaviour of the Lower Organisms* (Columbia University Press, 1905):

> While this exclusive use of objective terms has great advantages, it has one possible disadvantage. It seems to make an absolute gulf between the behavior of the lower organisms on the one hand, and that of man and higher animals on the other. From a discussion of the behavior of the lower organisms in objective terms, compared with a discussion of the behavior of man in subjective terms, we get the impression of complete discontinuity between the two.
>
> Does such a gulf actually exist, or does it lie only in our manner of speech? We can best get evidence on this question by comparing the objective features of behavior in lower and in higher organisms . . . (his p. 329)

After discussing the various reactions of a number of different protozoa, including the common ciliate *Paramecium*, he goes on as follows:

> But the question is sometimes proposed: Is the behavior of lower organisms of the character which we should 'naturally' expect and appreciate if they did have conscious states, of undifferentiated character, and acted under similar conscious states in a parallel way to man? Or is their behavior of such a character that it does not suggest to the observer the existence of consciousness?
>
> If one thinks these questions through for such an organism as paramecium, with all its limitations of

sensitiveness and movement, it appears to the writer that an affirmative answer must be given to the first of the above questions, and a negative one to the second. Suppose that this animal *were* conscious to such an extent as its limitations seem to permit. Suppose that it could feel a certain degree of pain when injured; that it received certain sensations from alkali, others from acids, others from solid bodies, etc., – would it not be natural for it to act as it does? . . . Still stronger, perhaps, is this impression when observing an amoeba obtaining food . . . The writer is thoroughly convinced, after long study of the behavior of this organism, that if amoeba were a large animal, so as to come within the everyday experience of human beings, its behavior would at once call forth the attribution to it of states of pleasure and pain, of hunger, desire, and the like, on precisely the same basis as we attribute these things to the dog . . . (his p. 336)

I am sure he is absolutely right, that simplest of all animals *amoeba* has many different methods of securing its food according to the life style of its prey; whilst it just engulfs a vegetable cell, it employs what can only be described in everyday language as stealth when capturing an active animal like a ciliate.

Polanyi's distinction between explicit and tacit knowledge marks the real division between man and the other animals, not consciousness. While we alone have the means of an explicit expression of our thoughts, and so the powers of logically discussing them with fellow members of our race, in the tacit emotional field there can be no sharp division between us and our animal ancestors.

Surely it is not unreasonable to suppose, as I have suggested, that the new habits which may develop in the higher animals, and lead to such behavioural selection as I have been discussing in the last chapter, may indeed be the result of their conscious exploratory actions. This is why I believe that

164

the concept of behavioural selection makes such a difference to our views on Darwinian evolution and its philosophical implications. We are not only one with the animal kingdom in a physico-chemical sense, we are one with it in our emotional life as well. On this emotional side, from the evidence of the records of their behaviour, can we doubt that animals experience conscious delight? Dolphins, which have been close companions in an oceanarium but then separated for a time, exhibit, when brought together again, such mutual excitement and exuberant play with one another that it must surely indicate conscious joy. Julian Huxley, in his *Memories* (1970, p. 61), describes how as a young man he first saw porpoises disporting themselves round the bows of a ship, 'obviously enjoying their leaping and racing, just as the herons at Avery Island which I saw some years later enjoyed their aerial flight-games. I realized how stupid the behaviourists were in denying any subjective emotional experience to animals.' Does not the delight of a dog on being taken out for a walk, or its expression of loyal devotion as it rests its head in our hands, show every appearance of a consciously felt emotion?

Where also, we may ask, do we draw the line, if indeed we must, between our spiritual life and the emotional side of animal behaviour? Such a question may seem outrageous, but let us pause for a moment before casting it aside. Animals, being without explicit thought and reasoning powers, can, of course, have no formulated ideas regarding anything like a religious concept; this is not what I mean. Under the headings of man's spiritual life, however, I would place in addition to his religious feelings, his joy in a quest or in the moment of discovery and his love of natural beauty and the arts. Whether animals have any appreciation of the beauty of their surroundings we have, of course, no means of knowing, and so perhaps a consideration of the arts seems irrelevant. However, what of man's love of adventure? Is not that perhaps linked with the restless, inquisitive, exploratory nature of animal life? Somehow, out of the process of evolution, has come the urge that drives a man to risk his life in climbing Everest, in reaching the South Pole or exploring the moon, just as in the past it sent more primitive men in frail canoes across the ocean. Is it altogether too naive to suggest that this drive, this curiosity, which is really at the heart of all true scientific seeking, has had its beginning in some deep-seated aspect of animal behaviour which has played a fundamental part in this process of life?

I have just said 'perhaps a consideration of the arts seems irrelevant'; going back to the last paragraph of Chapter 6 I have a hunch that just conceivably it isn't. I remember watching a television film of the private life of one of the Australian bower-birds, with that well-known artist, naturalist and man of action, Sir Peter Scott, acting as commentator. We saw the male bird placing a brightly coloured flower-petal into the decorated side of the bower through which he would later drive his mate during courtship stimulation. He put it into one position and then stood back looking at it for a moment with his head cocked on one side; then taking it up again he placed it in another position, and after having another look he went off apparently satisfied. 'Just as I do myself when painting a picture,' said Sir Peter, or words to that effect. There are, of course, some species of bower-birds which do actually 'paint' the branches forming the walls of their bower in bright colours from the juices of berries and fruits which they crush in their beaks, and at least one species uses a small wad of bark (like using a tool) to smear the stain on, as if with a paint-brush. This latter practice is described by A. J. Marshall in his book *Bower-Birds* (Oxford, 1954), p. 51. Again, do the female birds of paradise or tropical pheasants get only a sexual thrill when they see the glorious displays of their suitors, or is there an aesthetic element as well?

I hope I have said enough to suggest that Darwinian evolution need no longer be considered an entirely materialistic doctrine. It can only be so regarded if we either deny the part played by conscious behaviour or deem consciousness

166

itself to be no more than an illusory by-product of an entirely mechanistic system. I maintain that there is no reasonable support for the latter view and that to proclaim it as a part of well-established science is not only an unwarranted assumption or dogma but is a misrepresentation of the nature of life and of man, and so a danger to our civilization.

I will end this chapter by briefly quoting from the closing pages of *Living Organisms – An account of their Origin and Evolution* (Oxford, 1924) by that great zoologist Edwin S. Goodrich, F.R.S., who held the Linacre Chair at Oxford for some twenty-five years before I succeeded him. He wrote thus:

> Lastly, we are still in the dark as regards the evolution of consciousness, the highest stage in the development of the mental processes, for our knowledge of the anatomical structure and physico-chemical processes which accompany it is still too incomplete to enable us to determine when it first made its appearance in the animal series. . . .
>
> . . . It is useless to ask which is the more important in evolution, the mental or the physico-chemical series, since one cannot happen without the other, and they evolve *pari passu*.
>
> Too often the Darwinian doctrines are represented as teaching that success in the struggle for existence is obtained only by tooth and nail, by blood and iron. This is a very mistaken view. . . .

Then, writing of the human race, he says:

> Religion, art and science all play an important part in evolution; and morality appears not as an external force working against a ruthless and unmoral Cosmic Process, but as a product of that very process, and an all-important factor in its development.

9

A Change in Evolution

Although the process of evolution has been a continuous one, there has come about in a remarkably short period of time, geologically speaking, as great a change, or perhaps an even greater one, in the nature of life between man and his animal ancestors as that which distinguishes animals from plants. Man is an animal with a difference.

The purpose of this chapter is to discuss the nature and significance of this fundamental change which has come about in the evolution of man. Before proceeding to this, however, I think here may be as good a place as any in which to make good the promise I made in the introductory chapter (p. 13) to say a little more about Darwin's views about God and how they changed in later life; further, what he says, in the quotation I shall give, regarding the constant inculcation in a belief in God on the minds of children has a distinct relevance to Waddington's ideas which I shall refer to later in the chapter (p. 173).

In 1958 Charles Darwin's grand-daughter Nora Barlow (Lady Barlow) republished his autobiography with certain important original omissions restored. I now quote from a part of where he is relating how his ideas about God have changed, and show Nora Barlow's footnotes to explain the restoration of sentences which were removed by Mrs Darwin after his death:

Another source of conviction in the existence of God, connected with the reason and not with the feelings, impresses me as having much more weight. This fol-

168

lows from the extreme difficulty or rather impossibility of conceiving this immense and wonderful universe, including man with his capacity of looking far backwards and far into futurity, as the result of blind chance or necessity. When thus reflecting I feel compelled to look to a First Cause having an intelligent mind in some degree analogous to that of man; and I deserve to be called a Theist.

This conclusion[1] was strong in my mind about the time, as far as I can remember, when I wrote the *Origin of Species*; and it is since that time that it has very gradually with many fluctuations become weaker. But then arises the doubt – can the mind of man, which has, as I fully believe, been developed from a mind as low as that possessed by the lowest animal, be trusted when it draws such grand conclusions? May not these be the result of the connection between cause and effect which strikes us as a necessary one, but probably depends merely on inherited experience? Nor must we overlook the probability of the constant inculcation in a belief in God on the minds of children producing so strong and perhaps an inherited effect on their brains not yet fully developed, that it would be as difficult for them to throw off their belief in God, as for a monkey to throw off its instinctive fear and hatred of a snake.[2]

I cannot pretend to throw the least light on such abstruse problems. The mystery of the beginning of all things is insoluble by us; and I for one must be content to remain an Agnostic.

[1] Addendum of four lines added later. In Charles's MS. copy the interleaved addition is in his eldest son's hand. In Francis's copy it is in Charles's own hand. N.B.

[2] Added later. Emma Darwin wrote and asked Frank to omit this sentence when he was editing the Autobiography in 1885. The letter is as follows:

'Emma Darwin to her son Francis.   1885
My dear Frank,
There is one sentence in the Autobiography which I very much wish

I will now return to the real theme of the chapter: the great change that has come about in the main mode of evolution in man from that of the Darwinian system in the rest of the animal kingdom. This difference is the result of the extraordinarily rapid evolution of the brain, making possible a reasoning mind and the development of speech: the two faculties have indeed evolved hand in hand together as one process. Now here comes something even more surprising: the resulting powers of linguistic communication have altered the very mechanism of evolution itself. We are now within a different system from that governed simply by Darwinian natural selection.

Whilst we are still prone to the selective effects of pathogenic organisms and the effects of the physical environment, the force of these is continually being reduced by the progress of medicine and technology. Far more important now, in the evolution of human society, are the effects of traditions. The power of natural selection is being replaced by the acquisition of new knowledge and experience which is

---

to omit, no doubt partly because your father's opinion that *all* morality has grown up by evolution is painful to me; but also because where this sentence comes in, it gives one a sort of shock – and would give an opening to say, however injustly, that he considered all spiritual beliefs no higher than hereditary aversions or likings, such as the fear of monkeys towards snakes.

I think the disrespectful aspect would disappear if the first part of the conjecture was left without the illustration of the instance of monkeys and snakes. I don't think you need consult William about this omission, as it would not change the whole gist of the Autobiography. I should wish if possible to avoid giving pain to your father's religious friends who are deeply attached to him, and I picture to myself the way that sentence would strike them, even those so liberal as Ellen Tollett and Laura, much more Admiral Sullivan, Aunt Caroline, &c., and even the old servants.

Yours, dear Frank,

E.D.'

This letter appeared in *Emma Darwin* by Henrietta Litchfield in the privately printed edition from the Cambridge University Press in 1904. In John Murray's public edition of 1915 it was omitted. N.B.

handed on from generation to generation as well as being spread through the populations by speech, writing, the printed word and now by all the persuasive powers of the radio and television media. We have reached what Sir Julian Huxley called, in his Darwin centennial address at Chicago in 1959, the new psycho-social phase of evolution.

It was again that remarkable man Alfred Russel Wallace who was the first to point out this great change in evolution with the coming of man; I have recorded in Chapter 3 (p. 72) how he did so in 1864, seven years before Darwin wrote his *The Descent of Man*. I have quoted him at some length in that earlier chapter, but to save you looking back I will repeat a few small parts to remind you of the significance of what he was saying more than a hundred years ago; he wrote as follows:

> Thus man, by the mere capacity of clothing himself, and making weapons and tools, has taken away from nature that power of changing the external form and structure which she exercises over all other animals . . .
>
> From the time, therefore, when the social and sympathetic feelings came into active operation, and the intellectual and moral faculties became fairly developed, man would cease to be influenced by 'natural selection' in his physical form and structure; as an animal he would remain almost stationary; . . . his mind, however, would become subject to those very influences from which his body had escaped; every slight variation in his mental and moral nature . . . would be preserved and accumulated, . . . and that rapid advancement of mental organization would occur, which has raised the very lowest races of man so far above the brutes . . .

Surprise has sometimes been expressed that the languages of even the most primitive peoples of today are relatively well formed in their verbal structure, and that there are in fact no languages in the world which we might regard as being at a distinctly lower evolutionary level than others. By this I am meaning the structure of spoken language and not, of course, the production of literature as a creative and expressive art.[3] It would seem probable that when anything like a language developed from a more primitive communication by sounds and signs it would at once have great survival value; thus, as the form of primitive languages came under the influence of natural selection, those peoples with the less efficient forms of speech would continually tend to be eliminated and so all the early stages in the process would be lost. It would indeed be a part of what Wallace has referred to as 'that rapid advancement of mental organization'.

The significance of this great change in the nature of human evolution was well expressed by Sir Peter Medawar in his Reith Lectures (published as *The Future of Man*, 1960) in which he vividly brought home to us how relevant is a true knowledge of our own evolution for a proper understanding of human affairs.

> In their hunger for synthesis and systematization, the evolutionary philosophers of the nineteenth century and some of their modern counterparts have missed the point; they thought that great lessons were to be learnt from similarities between Darwinian and social evolution; but it is from the differences that all the great lessons are to be learnt. For one thing, our newer style of evolution is Lamarckian in nature. The environment cannot imprint genetical information upon us, but it can and does imprint non-genetical information which we can and do pass on. Acquired characters are indeed inherited. The blacksmith was under an illusion if he supposed [as Lamarck did] that his habits of life could impress themselves upon the genetic make-up of his children; but there is no doubting his ability to teach his

[3] A discussion of this, together with the views of various authorities, is given in C. H. Waddington's *The Ethical Animal* (Allen & Unwin, London, 1960), p. 145.

children his trade, so that they can grow up to be as stalwart and skilful as himself.

Earlier in his essays *The Uniqueness of the Individual* (1957, p. 141) he discusses the fundamental distinction between the 'springs of action' in mice and men. He points out that mice have no traditions, or at most very few as can be shown by breeding them in such a way that each individual in successive generations is separated from its parents from the moment of birth; when this is done there is 'no loss of their mouse-like ways'. He then makes his most telling point. 'The entire structure of human society as we know it,' he says, 'would be destroyed in a single generation if anything of the kind were to be done with man.' Tradition, he emphasizes, is 'a biological instrument, by means of which human beings conserve, propagate and enlarge upon those properties to which they owe their present biological fitness, and their hope of becoming fitter still.'

I will now draw attention to another side of this new phase of tradition in the evolution of man which had, I think, been largely overlooked until it was brought forward very forcibly by Professor C. H. Waddington in his book *The Ethical Animal*. He maintains that this new cultural system, the passing-on of acquired experience through the coming of speech can only work successfully, not merely if there is developed the means of offering the information to the new generation, but also if the *members of the new generation are made to receive it*. The new-born infant has, as he says, to be 'moulded into an information acceptor', in fact to be made 'ready to believe (in some general sense of the word) what it is told'. The mechanism of information transfer cannot work successfully until the human being has been turned by evolution into someone 'who goes in for believing'. He further points out that the development of an infant 'into an authority acceptor' – an entertainer of beliefs – 'involves the formation within his mind of some mental factors which carry authority, and that it is some aspects of these same authority-bearing systems that are responsible for his simultaneous moulding into an ethicizing creature'.

If what he is suggesting is true, and I must say that it seems to me most reasonable, then here is another important link between the biological system and the evolution of religion: the process of building into the mind of man a *capacity for belief*. We have been evolved into beings who tend to believe what we are told in our childhood. We are beings prone to be amenable to indoctrination, to take on trust what we are taught at our mother's knee, to be liable to become conditioned at an early age to any particular religious faith; it is all part of the new system of tradition, one of the latest developments in the long chain of biological evolution. Perhaps some may feel that this demonstration of the likely origin of the will to believe is yet another blow against religion, so let me say at once that, in the light of other evidence to be presented later, I do not feel this to be so at all – in fact the very reverse. It may well make us reconsider the significance of traditional dogmas; these, however, are not the essence of what I mean by a spiritual faith. And from what Waddington himself writes I think he would feel the same; in referring to the cultural development which differentiates our life today from that of our Stone-Age ancestors he says, 'It includes spiritual and intellectual changes as well as those concerning materials and tools.'

Another modern biologist who has stressed the great difference between the evolution of man and that of the rest of the animal kingdom is Richard Dawkins who in the final chapter of his vivid book *The Selfish Gene* (Oxford University Press, 1976) writes as follows:

The argument I shall advance, surprising as it may seem coming from the author of the earlier chapters, is that, for an understanding of the evolution of modern man, we must begin by throwing out the gene as the sole basis of our ideas on evolution. I am an enthusiastic Darwinian, but I think Darwinism is too big a theory to be

174

confined to the narrow context of the gene. The gene will enter my thesis as an analogy, nothing more.

What, after all, is so special about genes? The answer is that they are replicators.

Then after discussing the possibility of finding new methods of evolution – new replicators – on other planets, he continues:

> But do we have to go to distant worlds to find other kinds of replicators and other, consequent, kinds of evolution? I think that a new kind of replicator has recently emerged on this very planet. It is staring us in the face. It is still in its infancy, still drifting clumsily about in its primeval soup, but already it is achieving evolutionary change at a rate which leaves the old gene panting far behind.
>
> The new soup is the soup of human culture. We need a name for the new replicator, a noun which conveys the idea of a unit of cultural transmission, or a unit of *imitation*. 'Mimeme' comes from a suitable Greek root, but I want a monosyllable that sounds a bit like a 'gene'. I hope my classicist friends will forgive me if I abbreviate mimeme to *meme*. If it is any consolation, it could alternatively be thought of as being related to 'memory', or to the French word *même*. It should be pronounced to rhyme with 'cream'.
>
> Examples of memes are tunes, ideas, catch-phrases, clothes fashions, ways of making pots or of building arches. Just as genes propagate themselves in the gene pool by leaping from body to body via sperms or eggs, so memes propagate themselves in the meme pool by leaping from brain to brain via a process which, in the broad sense, can be called imitation.

Dawkins's concept of the new stage in evolution of the replicating memes – his 'new soup of human culture' – is somewhat reminiscent of the world of ideas and shared and transmitted thoughts which Pierre Teilhard de Chardin put forward in a very different book *The Phenomenon of Man* (translation by B. Wall, Collins, 1959) and called the noosphere. This is how Teilhard developed it:

> Geologists have for long agreed in admitting the zonal composition of our planet. We have already spoke of the barysphere, central and metallic, surrounded by the rocky lithosphere that in turn is surrounded by the fluid layers of the hydrosphere and the atmosphere. Since Suess, science has rightly become accustomed to add another to these four concentric layers, the living membrane composed of the fauna and flora of the globe, the biosphere . . .
>
> The recognition and isolation of a new era in evolution, the era of noogenesis, obliges us to distinguish . . . a new layer . . . the noosphere.

There can be little doubt, I think, that it was Teilhard's concept of the noosphere and all it stood for that excited Sir Julian Huxley so much and caused him to write the introduction to his book; it tied in so well with Huxley's ideas of the psycho-social phase of evolution which I have already mentioned (p. 171).

I should now make more reference to this remarkable book by Teilhard de Chardin: *The Phenomenon of Man* which was clutched at by so many with such thankfulness and enthusiasm because, with its introduction by Sir Julian, they thought that it must be a truly scientific book.

There can be no doubt that it is a book by a profoundly spiritual man who believes passionately that God must be linked with biological evolution. This indeed is an intuitive step in the right direction. In his preface, however, he says, 'If this book is to be properly understood it must be read not as a work of metaphysics, still less as a sort of theological essay, but purely and simply as a scientific treatise.' This I am afraid it certainly is not. I like to regard it as an imaginative prose poem of the emergence of the spirit of man and his feeling after divinity, but as science – *no*. In the development of his speculative scheme, he makes much play with the concept of energy having two forms which he proposes as a 'basis for all that is to emerge later'. In discussing 'the natural complexity of the stuff of the universe', he says that 'in each particular element this fundamental energy is divided into two distinct components: a *tangential energy* which links the element with others of the same order . . . and a *radial energy* which draws it towards ever greater complexity and centricity – in other words forwards'. These are not scientific concepts; in relation to this passage – on the same page (his p. 64) – it is interesting to note that there was for nearly ten years an extraordinary mistake which went unnoticed in the English and American editions of his book, where he is made to say that 'we shall assume that, essentially, all energy is physical in nature'. To many this must have seemed that he was here linking his ideas to orthodox science, whereas in the original French the word rendered as physical was not 'physique' but 'psychique'! It would appear that many of those who eagerly followed him quite misunderstood the real nature of his thesis. The error was not discovered until my book, *The Living Stream*, in which I had used this quotation from the English version, was being rendered into French; my translator was much shocked at this distortion of Teilhard's views.

Teilhard was certainly a saint and a true mystic who will, I believe, have a secure place in history with his spiritual classic, *Le Milieu Divin*, rather than with scientific theory; nevertheless his conception of God within the evolutionary process is indeed in line with the latest theological development – process theology.

In the chapters which follow we shall see the evidence which I believe will convince you that the deeper quality of the spirituality of man must be combined with Darwinian evolution to give an intellectually satisfying doctrine.

10

The Phenomenon of Faith

Whatever one's views may be regarding the nature of religion or spirituality no one can deny that such feelings have played a prominent part in the history of mankind. Edmund Burke in his *Reflections on the Revolution in France* so aptly wrote 'Man is by his constitution a religious animal'.

Let me here emphasize what I briefly pointed out in my Aberdeen lecture of 1942 which I quoted in Chapter 1 (p. 16). The wars of religion, or of rival ideologies, have been more bitter than those fought for economic ends. We are only too well aware of the terrible clashes between rival religious communities in the world today: between Hindu and Moslems in India and Pakistan; between Moslems and Jews in the Near East; and alas, between different sects of Christianity, Catholics and Protestants, in parts of our own country, Great Britain. Religion, primitive or sophisticated, in its many different forms, is indeed a part of human natural history; the emotions generated by such clashes can only be equalled in force by those of the jealousies of sex. This extraordinarily powerful element in life is surely worthy of just as much study as is sex; it is something quite different but as yet it is much less understood.

There is, I believe, no more important study to be undertaken by the intellectual world of today than this aspect of human natural history; it has been almost universal. Whilst I have stressed the need for its intellectual – academic – study, it must be recognized that the phenomenon itself is not a matter of reason but of emotion. As Pascal so well expressed it: 'The heart has its reasons that reason knows not of.' Many psychologists today would have us force these reasons of the heart into a framework of an entirely scientific explanation; I am sure this cannot be done, at any rate with science as we know it today. This is the great dilemma of our age; for a long time to come it must be the work not of scientists in the strict sense but of the observing naturalists. In the next chapter I shall be discussing the work of some of these pioneers; in the present one I illustrate the universality of such experience before coming to the actual study of it.

Apart from the example – the supreme example for Christians – of the New Testament, where in the literature of the world will we find man's realization of the divine spirit more beautifully expressed than in *The Book of Psalms*?

> Create in me a clean heart, O God;
> And renew a right spirit within me.
> Cast me not away from thy presence;
> And take not thy holy spirit from me.
> Restore unto me the joy of thy salvation;
>   And uphold me with thy free spirit.   *Psalm 51*[1]

> O God, thou art my God; early will I seek thee;
> My soul thirsteth for thee, my flesh longeth for thee
> In a dry and thirsty land, where no water is;
> To see thy power and thy glory,
> So as I have seen thee in the sanctuary.
> Because thy loving kindness is better than life,
> My lips shall praise thee.
> Thus will I bless thee while I live;
> I will lift up my hands in thy name.   *Psalm 63*[1]

Or let me take two examples from Christian writers:

Lord, make me an instrument of Thy Peace. Where there is hatred let me sow love; where there is injury, pardon; where there is doubt, faith; where there is

[1] From *The Bible designed to be read as Literature*, edited and arranged by Ernest Sunderland Bates.

179

despair, hope; where there is darkness, light; where there is sadness, joy.   *St Francis of Assisi*

Man ought to lay hold of God in everything, and he should train his mind to have God ever present in his thoughts, his intentions and affections.   *Meister Eckhart* (c. 1250–1328)

Or what of this early Stoic saying;

Lead me, O God, and I will follow, willingly if I am wise, but if not willingly I still must follow.

Or this from Epictetus:

Do with me henceforth as thou wilt. I am of one mind with Thee, I am Thine. I decline nothing that seems good to Thee. Send me whither you wilt. Clothe me as Thou wilt. Will Thou that I take office or live a private life, remain at home or go into exile, be poor or rich, I will defend Thy purpose with me in respect of all these.

Or if we turn to the Bhagavad-Gita of Hinduism we find:

God is seated in the hearts of all.

Or

Take our salutations, Lord, from every quarter,
Infinite of might and boundless in your glory,
You are all that is, since everywhere we find you . . .
Author of this world, the unmoved and the moving,
You alone are fit for worship, you the highest.
Where in the three worlds shall any find your equal?

Or again from the Sikhs, the dissenters from Brahmanical Hinduism, we find the following:

There is but one God, whose name is true, the Creator, devoid of fear and enmity, immortal, unborn, self-existent, great and bountiful. (From the *Japji*)

and

God is in my heart, yet thou searchest for him in the wilderness. (From the *Granth*)

Or take the writings of the Sufi poets of Islamic mysticism in Persia as exemplified by Jalalu D-Din Rumi:

What pearl art Thou, that no man may pay the price?
What doth the World offer, which is not a gift from Thee?
What punishment is greater, than to dwell afar from thy Face?
Torture not thy slave, tho' he be unworthy of Thee!

These examples are all taken from that beautiful anthology *God of a Hundred Names: Prayers of Many Peoples and Creeds* collected by Barbara Greene and Victor Gollancz (Gollancz, 1962). It is all summed up so well in the words of Mahatma Gandhi: (*Lamps of Fire*, Ed. J. Mascaro, 1961):

I claim to be a man of faith and prayer, and even if I were to be cut to pieces I trust God would give me the strength not to deny Him, but to assert that He is. The Mussulman says, 'He is, and there is no one else'. The Christian says the same thing, and so does the Hindu. If I may venture to say so, the Buddhist also says the same thing, only in different words. It is true that we may each of us be putting our own interpretation on the word 'God'. We must of necessity do so . . .

It is well to remember, in view of his opening sentence, that as he lay dying from the assassin's bullet his last words were 'He Ram! He Ram!' (Ah God! Ah God!).

In a more sophisticated way the same sentiments are expressed by Aldous Huxley in the opening paragraph of his *The Perennial Philosophy* (Chatto and Windus, London, 1947):

Philosophia perennis – the phrase was coined by Leibniz; but the thing – the metaphysic that recognizes a divine Reality substantial to the world of things and lives and minds; the psychology that finds in the soul something similar to, or even identical with, divine Reality; the ethic that places man's final end in the knowledge of the immanent and transcendent Ground of all being – the thing is immemorial and universal. Rudiments of the Perennial Philosophy may be found among the traditionary lore of primitive peoples in every region of the world, and in its fully developed forms it has a place in every one of the higher religions. A version of this Highest Common Factor in all preceding and subsequent theologies was first committed to writing more than twenty-five centuries ago, and since that time the inexhaustible theme has been treated again and again, from the standpoint of every religious tradition and in all the principal languages of Asia and Europe.

Aldous Huxley is referring to the main religious traditions of the world, but what of the religious feelings of the much more primitive peoples? Dr R. R. Marett, reader in social anthropology at Oxford in the early decades of the century, was the first to break away from the two leading ideas which dominated anthropology at the time: that of Sir James Frazer in his massive ten volume work *The Golden Bough* supposing that religion sprang from magic or that of Sir Edward Tyler in his *Primitive Culture* deriving it from animism, the cult of the worship of ancestral spirits. Whilst these elements no doubt appear in different forms of primitive religion, Marett found something much more important among primitive peoples all over the world; this was the recognition of a benign power beyond themselves, whether it was called *Mana* by the Polynesians, *Waken* by the North American Indians or by many other names by the various tribes of Africa. I will now give a little anthology of quotations to illustrate this from some of his works:

But enough has been said to show that, corresponding to the anthropologists' wide use of the term 'religion', there is a real sameness, felt all along if expressed with no great clearness at first, in the charactersitic manifestations of the religious consciousness at all times and in all places. It is the common experience of man that he can draw on a power that makes for, and in its most typical form wills, righteousness, the sole condition being that a certain fear, a certain shyness and humility, accompany the effort so to do. That such a universal belief exists amongst all mankind, and that it is no less universally helpful in the highest degree, is the abiding impression left on my mind by the study of religion in its historico-scientific aspect. (*Psychology and Folk-lore* 1920, p. 166.)

Or in another example:

A play of images sufficiently forcible to arouse by diffused suggestion a conviction that the tribal luck is taking a turn in the required direction is the sum of his theology; and yet the fact remains that a symbolism so gross and mixed can help the primitive man to feel more confident of himself – to enjoy the inward assurance that he is in touch with sources and powers of grace that can make him rise superior to the circumstances and chances of this mortal life. (*Head, Heart and Hands in Human Evolution* 1935, p. 17.)

Or again:

. . . religious observances of every kind would seem to have an absorbing quality of appeal that causes the participant to feel that for the moment he lives a life apart, is removed to another world. He is on a plane of existence where he seems to do hard things easily. Of course, he is more or less aware at the time that he is doing them symbolically, not actually. Even so, he now feels that he could do them as never before – that, given his present temper, they are as good as done . . . This new plane of experience is one baffling to the intellect because the literal, the language of the senses, no longer suffices; but it is apprehensible to the mind as a whole, since on the side of feeling and will the value of the dynamical mood approves itself directly. Herein, then, lies the truth of religious symbolism – not in what it says, for it speaks darkly, but in what it makes a man feel, namely, that his heart is strong.

There is much more of Marett that I would like to include, but I can give only one more quotation; it is from the ending paragraph of his lecture on 'Faith' in his Gifford Lectures *Faith, Hope and Charity in Primitive Religion* (1932):

. . . This revelation comes, however, to the primitive man in a special way. So concrete-minded is he that he is bound to be more or less of a pantheist. He encounters the divine stimulus here, there, and anywhere within the contents of an experience in which percepts play a far more important part than concepts. The civilized man, on the other hand, thanks to a far wider system of communications which entails a free use of mental symbols, favours a more abstract notion of deity, seeking to grasp it in the unity of its idea rather than in the plurality of its manifestations. Now in both these directions there lies danger, but in a different form. As for the savage, it is not a starved intellectualism that he has to fear, but on the contrary a sensualism nourished on a miscellaneous diet that is mixed up with a good deal of dirt. Yet, even though none of us may have reason to envy the child of nature either for his innocence, or for his digestion, the fact remains that he is uncritical of his rough fare and can extract from it all the rude health that a man can want. Whatever, then, may be the final judgement of ethics, a comparative history of morals is bound to assume that among the mixed ingredients of his religion the holiness prevails over the uncleanness, since the vital effect is to encourage him in a way of life that has a survival value. Thus, anthropologically viewed at all events, the faith of the savage is to be reckoned to him for righteousness.

Note that in his penultimate sentence he used the words 'a way of life that has survival value'. Here indeed is an important point; this feeling of a power beyond the self, giving strength and encouragement is now an evolutionary factor in man's behaviour. The primitive tribes who have their faith in this power are apt to be the more successful.

Quite independently Émile Durkheim, the great French sociologist, was coming to very similar views regarding primitive religion but he regarded it as an eminently social-collective phenomenon. I quote from his *Elementary Forms of Religious Life* (trans. J. Swain 1915):

> . . . The believer, who has communicated with his god, is not merely a man who sees new truths of which the unbeliever is ignorant; he is a man who is *stronger*. He feels within him more force, either to endure the trials of existence, or to conquer them. It is as though he were raised above the miseries of the world, because he is raised above his condition as a mere man; he believes that he is saved from evil, under whatever form he may conceive this evil. The first article in every creed is the belief in salvation by faith . . .
>
> Our entire study rests upon this postulate that the unanimous sentiment of the believers of all times cannot be purely illusory. Together with a recent apologist of the faith [he is referring here to William James] we admit that these religious beliefs rest upon a specific experience whose demonstrative value is, in one sense, not one bit inferior to that of scientific experiments, though different from them.

He goes on to say much more about the development of religion as a social force. Many seem to have thought that his theory of religion is one linking it to a simply *mechanistic* interpretation of the evolution of man as a social animal.

Nothing could be further from the truth, as is clearly shown by his following statement:

> . . . it is necessary to avoid seeing in this theory of religion a simple restatement of historical materialism: that would be misunderstanding our thought to an extreme degree. In showing that religion is something essentially social, we do not mean to say that it confines itself to translating into another language the material forms of society and its immediate vital necessities. It is true that we take it as evident that social life depends upon its material foundation and bears its mark, just as the mental life of an individual depends upon his nervous system and in fact his whole organism. But collective consciousness is something more than a mere epiphenomenon of its morphological basis, just as individual consciousness is something more than a simple efflorescence of the nervous system . . .

One last quotation from Durkheim and I must leave this mine of fascinating ideas:

> In summing up, then, we must say that society is not at all the illogical or a-logical, incoherent and fantastic being which it has too often been considered. Quite on the contrary, the collective consciousness is the highest form of the psychic life, since it is the consciousness of the consciousnesses.

It seems to me that there is more than a slight similarity between the 'collective consciousness' of Durkheim and that of C. G. Jung, but I must not develop the theme here.

The work of two quite outstanding anthropologists who have studied the religion of primitive peoples I shall reserve for the next chapter: the late Sir Edward Evans-Pritchard and Dr Godfrey Lienhardt; they more than any others may indeed be called the observing naturalists of primitive religion, for they have lived with the people they have been studying and got to know their real feelings and attitudes.

In my introductory chapter I referred to the sociobiological approach being pioneered by Professor Edward O. Wilson in America. It is indeed good to see the importance he attaches to the phenomenon of religion in human society; in his book *On Human Nature* he writes as follows:

> The predisposition to religious belief is the most complex and powerful force in the human mind and in all probability an ineradicable part of human nature. Emile Durkheim, an agnostic, characterized religious practice as the consecration of the group and the core of society. It is one of the universals of social behaviour, taking recognizable form in every society from hunter-gatherer bands to socialist republics. Its rudiments go back at least to the bone altars and funerary rites of Neanderthal man . . . [I should point out here that Wilson is wrong in calling Durkheim an agnostic; whilst he did not believe in an anthropomorphic deity, he was, as seen in the quotations given, a most positive believer in, as he says, 'salvation by faith'.]
>
> Skeptics continue to nourish the belief that science and learning will banish religion, which they consider to be no more than a tissue of illusions. The noblest among them are sure that humanity migrates towards knowledge by logotaxis, an automatic orientation toward information, so that organized religion must continue its retreat as darkness before enlightenment's brightening dawn. But this conception of human nature, with roots going back to Aristotle and Zeno, has never seemed so futile as today. If anything, knowledge is being enthusiastically harnessed to the service of religion. The United States, technologically and scientifically the most sophisticated nation in history, is also the second most religious – after India. According to a Gallup poll taken in 1977, 94 per cent of Americans believe in God or some form of higher being, while 31 per cent have undergone a moment of sudden religious

insight or awakening, their brush with the epiphany. The most successful book in 1975 was Billy Graham's *Angels: God's Secret Messengers*, which sold 810,000 hard-cover copies.

A little later he says:

> I suggest that the paradox can be at least intellectually resolved, not all at once but eventually and with consequences difficult to predict, if we pay due attention to the sociobiology of religion. Although the manifestations of the religious experience are resplendent and multi-dimensional, and so complicated that the finest of psychoanalysts and philosophers get lost in their labyrinth, I believe that religious practices can be mapped onto the two dimensions of genetic advantage and evolutionary change.
>
> Let me moderate this statement at once by conceding that if the principles of evolutionary theory do indeed contain theology's Rosetta stone, the translation cannot be expected to encompass in detail all religious phenomena. By traditional methods of reduction and analysis science can explain religion but cannot diminish the importance of its subtance.

Where I differ from E. O. Wilson can well be illustrated by my quoting from the concluding paragraphs to his chapter on religion in which he writes:

> The scientist's devotion to parsimony in explanation excludes the divine spirit and other extraneous agents. Most importantly, we have come to the crucial stage in the history of biology when religion itself is subject to the explanations of the natural sciences. As I have tried to show, sociobiology can account for the very origin of mythology by the principle of natural selection acting on the genetically evolving material structure of the human brain.

188

If this interpretation is correct, the final decisive edge enjoyed by scientific naturalism will come from its capacity to explain traditional religion, its chief competitor, as a wholly material phenomenon.

Science, by its very nature, cannot be dogmatic but scientists themselves are, I fear, often so; such dogmatism must, however, give way before the great accumulation of observations now being brought together as we shall see. In the quotation above we see Wilson extolling the scientist's devotion to parsimony in explanation which makes him reject such agents that do not fit into his theoretical schema instead of examining and weighing up the evidence for or against their reality. He has indeed done well in emphasizing the importance of religion in human culture since the earliest times, but I cannot myself subscribe to a sociobiology which depends upon the elimination of those factors which prove to be inconvenient for a biology entirely limited to the physio-chemical study of life. My own sociobiology, if I may call it such, which I outlined over forty years ago (see p. 17) was very different.

A few weeks before writing this chapter Mr David Hay, a lecturer in biology in the School of Education in the University of Nottingham and director of a religious experience research project gave three short talks in the BBC's 'Thought for the Day' series: with his kind permission I will end this chapter with a brief quotation from the beginning of his first talk. It is another fine example of the universality of religion. He introduces the same theme in the opening of his recent exciting book *Exploring Inner Space: Scientists and Religious Experience*, Penguin Books, 1982. I shall be discussing his work in the next two chapters. This is how he begins his talk:

In 1519 a band of Spanish adventurers led by Herman Cortes landed on the Mexican coast for the first time. They rushed inland until they came to the great city of Tenochtitlan with its huge stone-built temples, its great causeways and streets bustling with people and its complex administration and social hierarchy. The Spaniards were confronting Aztec civilization.

Cortes began to do what all invading conquerors seem to do: he imposed his values and beliefs on the people he was attempting to subdue. One of his first acts was to overturn the statues of the Aztec gods and roll them down the stairs of the temples. In their place he set up images of the Virgin Mary and other Christian saints. This upset the Aztecs a great deal, because they believed they owed their existence and well-being to their gods.

What is fascinating about this is that two cultures, separated from each other for tens of thousands of years, should share a mutually recognizable belief in their dependence on a supernatural power or powers. That is why Cortes knew where to set up the images of the saints.

Ever since Cortes' time there has been a steady stream of information coming back to Europe from adventurers, missionaries and more recently, anthropologists, showing that religious belief is almost universal amongst the human species. It forms the heart of every great historical culture without exception and is so common in tribal societies that anthropologists usually doubt the quality of their field work if they fail to find it.

David Hay's illustration of the coming together of those two civilizations which had been separated by some tens of thousands of years is indeed a vivid example of the universality of the phenomenon of faith as a part of the nature of man. We proceed in the next chapter to make a special study of some of the work of the more prominant observers of this side of human behaviour.

11

Naturalists of the Numinous

In earlier chapters I have stressed the importance of the observations of the great field naturalists of the last century in providing the evidence for the theory of evolution; it was these naturalists, *not* the laboratory biologists, who changed the outlook of the world. It will, I believe, be the observers and recorders of human experience who in this century will have a similar effect, but in a different direction: convincing the intellectual world of man's spiritual nature.

The two great pioneers in this naturalist-like study of human nature were both Americans: Professor Edwin Starbuck of Stanford University who published his *The Psychology of Religion, an Emperical Study of the Growth of Religious Consciousness* in 1899 and Professor William James of Harvard University who gave the Gifford Lectures in Edinburgh, which were published in 1902 as *The Varieties of Religious Experience, a Study in Human Nature*. They were the founder figures of a new revolution in thought, just as Darwin and Wallace were in relation to evolution. Whilst there can be no doubt, I think, from the depth of his vision and philosophy that James must be considered the greater of the two, we should not forget that Starbuck was the originator; without him we should never have had James's *Varieties*. In his foreword to his own book James thanks Starbuck for making over to him 'his large collection of manuscript material', and throughout his work he draws extensively upon these examples; this, however, was by no means all that James owed to Starbuck for he was in fact converted by him to quite a new approach to the study of religious experience as we may see from the remarkable preface he wrote to the latter's book which is worthy of full quotation:

Many years ago Dr Starbuck, then a student in Harvard University, tried to enlist my sympathies in his statistical inquiry into the religious ideas and experiences of the circumambient population. I fear that to his mind I rather damned the whole project with my words of faint praise. The question-circular method of collecting information had already, in America, reached the proportions of an incipient nuisance in psychological and pedagogical matters. Dr Starbuck's questions were of a peculiarly searching and intimate nature, to which it seemed possible that an undue number of answers from egotists lacking in sincerity might come. Moreover, so few minds have the least spark of originality that answers to questions scattered broadcast would be likely to show a purely conventional content. The writers' ideas, as well as their phraseology, would be the stock-in-trade of the Protestant Volksgeist, historically and not psychologically based; and, being in it one's self, one might as well cipher it all out *a priori* as seek to collect it in this burdensome, inductive fashion. I think I said to Dr Starbuck that I expected the chief result of his circulars would be a certain number of individual answers relating peculiar experiences and ideas in a way that might be held as typical. The sorting and extracting of percentages and reducing to averages, I thought, would give results of comparatively little significance.

But Dr Starbuck kept all the more resolutely at his task, which has involved an almost incredible amount of drudging labour. I have handled and read a large proportion of his raw material, and I have just finished reading the revised proofs of the book. I must say that the results amply justify his own confidence in his methods, and that I feel somewhat ashamed at present of the littleness of my own faith.

The material, quite apart from the many acutely interesting individual confessions which it contains, is evidently sincere in its general mass. The Volksgeist of course dictates its special phraseology and most of its conceptions, which are almost without exception Protestant, and predominantly of the Evangelical sort; and for comparative purposes similar collections ought yet to be made from Catholic, Jewish, Mohammedan, Buddhist and Hindoo sources . . .

But it has been Dr Starbuck's express aim to disengage the general from the specific and local in this critical discussion, and to reduce the reports to their most universal psychological value. It seems to me that here the statistical method has held its own, and that its percentages and averages have proved to possess genuine significance . . .

James ends his preface by saying that Dr Starbuck 'has broken ground in a new place . . . and that the enquiry ought to be extended to other lands and to populations of other faiths'.

I will now quote from the stirring opening to Starbuck's book; he writes thus:

Science has conquered one field after another, until now it is entering the most complex, the most inaccessible, and, of all, the most sacred domain – that of religion. The Psychology of Religion has for its work to carry the well-established methods of science into the analysis and organisation of the facts of the religious consciousness, and to ascertain the laws which determine its growth and character.

. . . It is scarcely questioned at the present time that all our mental processes follow an orderly sequence. We go one step further, and affirm that there is no event in the spiritual life which does not occur in accordance with immutable laws. The study of religion is today where astronomy and chemistry were four centuries ago. The world has been taken away from the oracle, alchemist, astrologer and petty gods, and given over to the control of law. Another four hundred years may restore to law the soul of man, with all its hopes, aspirations and yearnings.

He emphasizes that his study is one on 'the line of growth in religion in individuals and an enquiry into the causes and conditions which determine it'. His method is to analyze a vast number of records which he obtained as answers to a somewhat elaborate questionnaire sent out to a large number of people. For the greater part he is comparing the emotional feelings of those who during adolescence undergo a sudden conversion and those who have a more gradual development without any such dramatic metamorphosis. What comes out so clearly in the former is the organization of life about a new centre which brings with it two important results: the lifting up of the personality into greater significance and the sense of newness with which the whole world of objects is viewed – a sense of having discovered reality. The person involved appears to have a new feeling of the possession of things and participation in them.

Starbuck goes on to show how, in classifying the facts of the changed relation to the world, they fell into three groups depending on the subject of attachment: to persons, to nature, and to God or Christ. Of the first such examples, as 'I began to work for others; immediately I was anxious that all should experience the same'; or 'I felt for everyone, and loved my friends better'; or 'I felt everyone to be my friend', etc. In relation to nature: 'I had a special feeling of reverence towards nature'; 'I seemed to see God's greatness in nature', etc. In relation to God or Christ: A girl of 11: 'God was not afar off; he was my father and Christ my elder brother'; a girl of 14: 'Fear of God was gone; I saw he was the greatest friend one can have'; a boy of 14: 'I felt very near to my God'; a boy of 15: 'I felt in harmony with everybody, and all creation and its creator'. Starbuck summarizes these results in a table showing the *percentage* of cases in which a changed relation to God, nature and persons was mentioned as a result of conversion as follows:

	Females	Males
Desire to help others	28	28
Love for others	42	42
Closer relation to Nature	31	34
Closer relation to God	43	43
Closer relation to Christ	6	4

It is seen how remarkably similar are the results for the two sexes. Starbuck points out that these percentages express the lowest possible estimate since they represent only the number of cases in which the phenomenon was sufficiently prominent to receive explicit mention. Those feeling a closer relation to God form nearly fifty per cent of the cases if we add those specifically mentioning Christ; it seems reasonable to do this when we remember that those asked were definitely in a Christian community so that the majority would regard Christ as equal to God. It is interesting that a third of them felt the closer relation to nature; Otto refers to this in his study of the numinous which we shall consider later (p. 206).

It is clear from the table, as he says, 'that in a large per cent of cases an immediate result of conversion is to call the person out of himself into active sympathy with the world outside'. Following his treatment of the phenomenon of conversion Starbuck has a corresponding study of religious development which does not involve any such sudden change. He shows that this gradual-growth type is usually just as definite as that of the conversion type. The persons concerned are generally as capable of self-analysis, but for them there are no sudden crises which mark the disappearance of an old life and the beginning of a new one. He now proceeds to present his results in a series of statistical tables and graphs, for which I have not the space to reproduce; finally he goes on to an analysis of *adult* religious feelings, about which he says: 'Provided the cases we are studying are typical, the line along which religion grows, when represented in terms of feeling, is expressed as dependence, reverence, sense of oneness with God, and faith.'

We must now pass to William James. His *Varieties of Religious Experience* is perhaps the greatest single contribution yet made in the scientific spirit to the natural history of man's religious life. Whilst much of it, too much perhaps, deals with the more abnormal side of man's religious development, he sketches out a broad chart of the field and presents his own conclusions. The fact that various psychologists and philosophers have so many different ways of conceiving what religion is, relating it to dependence, fear, sex, the feeling of the infinite and so on, should, he says, make us doubt whether what is called the 'religious sentiment' can really be one specific thing; he regards it as a collective term, embracing many sentiments which may be aroused in alternation, and sees in it nothing of a psychologically specific nature.

Later on (his p. 53) he says that 'were one asked to characterize the life of religion in the broadest and most general terms possible, one might say that it consists of the belief that there is an unseen order, and that our supreme good lies in harmoniously adjusting ourselves thereto'.

After giving a number of examples of the feeling of God's close presence, he goes on to discuss 'the convincingness of these feelings of reality'. They are, he maintains, as convincing to those who have them as any direct sensible experience can be and are usually much more convincing than 'results established by mere logic ever are'. In discussing the opposition in philosophy between such mysticism and rationalism, we see the importance which he himself placed on the subconscious mind before the influence of Freud; after praising the rationalistic system for giving us among other good things the fruits of physical science, he says:

If you have intuitions at all they come from a deeper level of your nature than the loquacious level which rationalism inhabits. Your whole subconscious life, your impulses, your faiths, your needs, your divinations, have prepared the premises, of which your consciousness now feels the weight of the result; and something in you absolutely knows that that result must be truer than any logic-chopping rationalistc talk, however clever, that may contradict it.

James wrote a great deal about the subconscious although he often called it the subliminal mind, taking the phrase from F. W. H. Myers who – again before Freud – spoke of a threshold (limen) of consciousness, a level above which sensation and thought must rise before it can enter into our conscious life. 'Perceiving', said Myers, 'that these submerged thoughts and emotions possess the characteristics which we associate with conscious life I feel bound to speak of a subliminal consciousness.' Myers developed his ideas particularly in relation to psychical research, whereas James, although deeply interested in that subject, was specially concerned with the bearings of the subliminal mind upon religion. 'In it', he writes (p. 424), 'arise whatever mystical experiences we may have . . . In persons deep in the religious life, as we have now abundantly seen – and this is my conclusion – the door into this region seems unusually wide open; at any rate, experiences making their entrance through that door have had emphatic influence in shaping religious history.'

James has much to say regarding two types, the 'healthy-minded' and the 'sick soul', sometimes referring to them by the terms (used by Francis Newman)[1] the once-born and twice-born. 'In their extreme forms . . . the two types', he says, 'are violently contrasted . . .' but those 'human beings whom we oftenest meet are intermediate varieties and mixtures.' It is just the same with Jung's psychological types of

[1] Brother of Cardinal Newman.

extroversion and introversion, and indeed they are most likely related, as suggested by Professor Grensted. By the extrovert Jung meant, of course, the more outward-looking individual mainly interested in the outer objective world, and the other, the introvert, is the more inward-looking person, turned in upon himself to dwell more upon his own subjective feeling. In giving examples of the state of the sick soul James quotes extracts from Tolstoy and Bunyan and points out that they could and did find something welling up within them by which such extreme sadness could be overcome: 'a stimulus, an excitement, a faith, a force that re-infuses the positive willingness to live'.

It is, of course, impossible in just a few paragraphs to do more than suggest something of the sweep and scope of James's book; in leading up to his conclusions I will quote an earlier passage where he has again been discussing the subconscious. After declaring that the whole development of Christianity in inwardness has consisted in the greater and greater emphasis attached to the crisis of self-surrender, he goes on to say (on p. 211):

> Psychology and religion are thus in perfect harmony up to this point, since both admit that there are forces seemingly outside of the conscious individual that bring redemption to his life. Nevertheless psychology, defining these forces as 'subconscious', and speaking of their effects as due to 'incubation', or 'cerebration', implies that they do not transcend the individual's personality; and herein she diverges from Christian theology, which insists that they are direct supernatural operations of the Deity. I propose to you that we do not yet consider this divergence final, but leave the question for a while in abeyance . . .

Here James touches on what is surely the most important issue. Do these forces which play so vital a part in man's religious life belong only to his subconscious mind or do they indicate some extra-sensory contact with some power beyond the self? That is the question. If the findings of so-called parapsychology should come to be recognized as true – if they should indicate that mental activity does indeed extend beyond the localized mind, either conscious or subconscious – would they lend any support to the latter view? It is these 'if's' that are so tantalizing.

Towards the end, after discussing mysticism and the more psychological and philosophical aspects of his subject, James returns to this crucial problem – do those religious forces, or do they not, transcend the individual's personality? He writes:

> . . . confining ourselves to what is common and generic, we have in *the fact that the conscious person is continuous with a wider self through which saving experiences come*, a positive content of religious experience which, it seems to me, *is literally and objectively true as far as it goes*. If I now proceed to state my own hypothesis about the farther limits of this extension of our personality, I shall be offering my own over-belief . . .
>
> The further limits of our being plunge, it seems to me, into an altogether other dimension of existence from the sensible and merely 'understandable' world. Name it the mystical region, or the supernatural region, whichever you choose. So far as our ideal impulses originate in this region . . . we belong to it in a more intimate sense than that in which we belong to the visible world, for we belong in the most intimate sense wherever our ideals belong. Yet the unseen region in question is not merely ideal, for it produces effects in this world. When we commune with it, work is actually done upon our finite personality, for we are turned into new men, and consequences in the way of conduct follow in the natural world upon our regenerative change . . . But that which produces effects within another reality must be termed a reality itself, so I feel as

if we had no philosophic excuse for calling the unseen or mystical world unreal.

God is the natural appellation, for us Christians at least, for the supreme reality, so I will call this higher part of the universe by the name of God. [His p. 515, italics in the original.]

At the very end of his book James added a philosophical postscript which represents his summing-up after he has examined so many examples of different people's religious experience. In it he writes:

If asked just where the differences in fact which are due to God's existence come in, I should have to say that in general I have no hypothesis to offer beyond what the phenomenon of 'prayerful communion', especially when certain kinds of incursion from the subconscious region take part in it, immediately suggests. The appearance is that in this phenomenon something ideal, which in one sense is part of ourselves and in another sense is not ourselves, actually exerts an influence, raises our centre of personal energy and produces regenerative effects unattainable in other ways . . . I am so impressed by the importance of these phenomena that I adopt the hypothesis which they so naturally suggest. At these places at least, I say, it would seem as though transmundane energies, God, if you will, produced immediate effects within the natural world to which the rest of our experience belongs.

Here he picks out the same factor that has been so prominent in the accounts of primitive religion: that power of influence, call it what we will, that 'raises our centre of personal energy, and produces regenerative effects unattainable in other ways'. Now let us compare this statement with one made by another psychologist, Professor Sir Frederic Bartlett of Cambridge, who was giving the Riddell Memorial Lectures in 1950, nearly half a century after James's Gifford Lectures:

I confess that I cannot see how anybody who looks fairly at a reasonable sample of actions claiming a religious sanction can honestly refuse to admit that many of them could not occur, or at least that it is highly improbable that they would occur in the forms in which they do, if they were simply the terminal points of a psychological sequence, every item in which belonged to our own human, day-to-day world. I am thinking not of the dramatic and extraordinary actions which people who write books about religion mostly seem to like to bring forward. They are rare anyway. I remember the ways of life of many unknown and humble people whom I have met and respected. It seems to me that these people have done, effectively and consistently, many things which all ordinary sources of evidence seem to set outside the range of unassisted humanity. When they say 'It is God working through me', I cannot see that I have either the right or the knowledge to reject their testimony.

To the naturalist who has an open mind and is not tied to the dogmas of either materialism or theology it may well seem significant that there is an extraordinary similarity in the nature of religion in its simplest form among whatever people – primitive or sophisticated – it may be found. Here is some factor in human life that appears to have a profound effect, something which, if man responds to it, provides him with a power over his difficulties that he might not otherwise have and gives him a feeling of confidence and courage in the face of adversity. Is not this very different from being only a reinforcement of a social code? I do not for a moment deny that religion has often been used as such a reinforcement; what I am suggesting is that fundamentally it has a much deeper significance.

It might have been expected that the work of these two great pioneers in the study of religious experience, Starbuck and James, would have been followed by others in the religious field to provide us with a new, more realistic, natural theology; no one, however, followed them except the social anthropologists studying the religious feelings of the more primitive peoples. I have already discussed the work of Marett and Durkheim in the last chapter, but I now come to those other two quite outstanding examples of observers whom I also mentioned, Pritchard and Lienhardt, but reserved them for this chapter as the real naturalists. They went to live with the tribes they studied and got to know them so well that they could analyze their thoughts and behaviour to a remarkable degree. The peoples they studied are neighbouring, cattle-herding tribes, the Dinka and the Nuer, of the Southern Sudan. I doubt if there exist any more careful studies of the intimate religious life of social groups of present-day people than the accounts of these two tribes; indeed, I doubt the existence of any comparable studies; not since, I believe, the remarkable records of the tribes of Israel in the Old Testament have we had anything like them. Through the painstaking work of two eminent social anthropologists we now know more of the religious feelings of these particular people than we do of those of any social communities, either urban or rural, in our modern western society. Just as the researches of the students of animal behaviour are showing us the springs of action of animals living under natural conditions, so it is that these examples of field anthropology are illuminating for us the nature of religious experience in its unsophisticated state. Among the Dinka and Nuer tribes we find religion developed apparently from their own experience and not by contamination from external missionary sources. In just a few paragraphs it is impossible, of course, to give anything more than the merest sketch of the nature of their religious life, but enough, I hope, to indicate its significance for our discussion; these two pieces of field research are, I believe, key studies in the development of our natural-history approach to the idea of God.

I will take the Dinka religion first because it is, I feel, not so highly developed as that of the Nuer; the study was made by Dr Godfrey Lienhardt, lecturer in African sociology at Oxford, and published in his book, *Divinity and Experience: The Religion of the Dinka* (Clarendon Press, Oxford) in 1961. The essence of their religion is the existence of a spiritual element which they encounter in many different forms in their surroundings and life; Lienhardt calls them powers rather than spirits, for they are not to be thought of as forming a separate 'spirit-world' of their own. The Dinka think in terms of a broad division into 'that which is of men' and 'that which is of powers', and their religion is concerned with the inter-relations of these two different natures in the single world of their own experience. When talking about their religion they most frequently use a word (*nhialic*) which literally means 'up' or 'above' and may sometimes be used for 'the sky', but it is also referred to as 'creator' and 'father', and prayers and sacrifices are offered to it. For some purposes it could well be translated as God, yet this, as Dr Lienhardt points out, will hardly do, for while it is used sometimes to mean a supreme being, it can also denote the collective activity of a multiplicity of beings; he therefore translates it as Divinity.

This seems to be the core of Dinka religion – the belief that their world of experience is permeated with Divinity; it is, Lienhardt says, concerned with 'a relationship between men and ultra-human powers, between the two parts of a radically divided world'. Although they speak of sky-powers, for them Divinity is one; if they knew what it meant, they would, says Lienhardt (p. 156), 'deeply resent being described as "polytheistic". And again he says (p. 157), 'Divinity . . . transcends the individual . . . This theme is frequently stressed in Dinka invocations and hymns:

> . . . and you, Divinity, I call you in my invocation because you help everyone and you are great towards [in relation to] all people, and all people are your children . . .'

Here then we again find this feeling of receiving help from a power, from Divinity, beyond the self.

The religion of the neighbouring tribe, the Nuer, examined with so much understanding by Professor Sir Edward Evans-Pritchard in his book, *Nuer Religion* (1956), has developed on to a higher and more philosophical plane than that of the Dinka. With the Nuer individual prayer and communication with the Deity is a common practice, whereas for the Dinka, who as a rule make group supplications, individual prayer is a rarity. It is indeed extraordinary that the Nuer, with so simple a culture, should have reached such a high level in their religion and that they should, as far as we know, have done so quite independently of any contact with Judaism or with Christian influences. Their philosophy, essentially of a religious kind, 'is dominated by the idea of *Kwoth*, Spirit'. This, as it cannot be directly experienced by the senses, is defined by them only by referring to its effects and by the use of symbols and metaphors. If the Nuer are asked what Spirit is thought to be like in itself, they make no claim to know. 'They say', writes Sir Edward, 'that they are merely *doar*, simple people, and how can simple people know about such matters? What happens in the world is determined by Spirit and Spirit can be influenced by prayer and sacrifice. This much they know, but no more; and they say, very sensibly, that since the European is so clever perhaps he can tell them the answer to the question he asks.'

He goes on to discuss different aspects of Nuer religion, and a little later (p. 317) says:

> We can say that these characteristics . . . of Nuer religion indicate a distinctive kind of piety which is dominated by a strong sense of dependence on God and confidence in him rather than in any human powers or endeavours. God is great and man foolish and feeble, a tiny ant. And this sense of dependence is remarkably individualistic. It is an intimate, personal relationship between man and God . . . In prayer and sacrifice alike,

in what is said and in what is done, the emphasis is on complete surrender to God's will.

The final paragraph of his book is of particular interest for us:

> We can, therefore, say no more than that Spirit is an intuitive apprehension, something experienced in response to certain situations but known directly only to the imagination and not to the senses . . . Hands are raised to the sky in supplication, but it is not the sky which is supplicated but what it represents to the imagination . . . If we regard only what happens in sacrifice before the eyes it may seem to be a succession of senseless, and even cruel and repulsive acts, but when we reflect on their meaning we perceive that they are a dramatic representation of a spiritual experience . . . Though prayer and sacrifice are exterior actions, Nuer religion is ultimately an interior state. This state is externalized in rites which we can observe, but their meaning depends finally on an awareness of God and that men are dependent on him and must be resigned to his will.

In any study of religion mention must be made of the concept which the German theologian, Rudolf Otto, called the numinous. He wrote on it at length in his book, *Das Heilige*, published in 1917 (translated as *The Idea of the Holy*, Oxford University Press, London, 1923). Since it has had considerable influence in theological circles I think it well to point out that it is not something only experienced by those embracing the more sophisticated faiths; it appears to be something much more primitive, as has been shown by the social anthropologists. For Otto, the numinous has an objective reality and should not, he says, be regarded as a subjective feeling in the mind; when he speaks of the feeling of the numinous he really means a form of awareness which he would say was neither that of ordinary perceiving nor ordinary conceiving, but a peculiar apprehension of this mystical something – the numinous. He insists that it is not itself an emotion like an effective feeling of love, joy or fear; it is something which, he says,

> . . . is to be found, in the lives of those around us, in sudden, strong ebullitions of personal piety . . . in the fixed and ordered solemnities of rites and liturgies, and again in the atmosphere that clings to old religious monuments and buildings, to temples and to churches . . . we shall find we are dealing with something for which there is only one appropriate expression, 'mysterium tremendum'. The feeling of it may at times come sweeping like a gentle tide, pervading the mind with a tranquil mood of deepest worship.

Having quoted Otto's views, we should not forget that William James, writing earlier, expressed this somewhat differently. He stressed that whilst we speak of religious love, religious fear, religious awe, or joy or so forth, they are only man's natural emotions directed to a religious object: for example, he says, 'religious awe is the same organic thrill we shall feel in a forest at twilight or in a mountain gorge; only this time it comes over us at the thought of our supernatural relations. Returning to Otto we should recall that in an appendix to his English edition (p. 215) he quoted a remarkable passage from Ruskin describing an experience in his youth felt whilst on the banks of a mountain stream which made him 'shiver from head to foot with the joy and fear of it'; these experiences, says Otto, 'are purely numinous in character'.

In the title of this chapter I have used the phrase 'Naturalists of the Numinous' to describe the work of some of the great pioneers in making the observational approach to the study of man's experience. I will now proceed in the next chapter to discuss the results coming from a special research unit set up to make this naturalist's approach to the study of thousands of examples of personal records of such spiritual awareness.

12

Research and its Results

At the end of my second series of Gifford Lectures, published as *The Divine Flame* (Collins, 1966), I announced my intention of founding what I proposed to call the Religious Experience Research Unit at Manchester College, Oxford. It was established in 1969 to study the nature of such experience among the population of the present-day world. From an examination of thousands of examples we have built up the beginnings of a natural history of this side of man.

We began collecting our material by a series of articles and appeals for such records in the general press. It is impossible, of course, to make a direct examination of the actual subjective feelings of the people concerned, but we can indeed make an objective study of their *written* accounts of such experience, and this is what we have done. We asked all those who had felt they had been conscious of, and perhaps influenced by, some power, whether they called it God or not, which had appeared to them to be either beyond their individual selves or partly or even entirely within their being, to write as simple a description of these feelings and their effects as they could. They were then asked to include particulars of age, sex, nationality, religious upbringing and other factors thought to be relevant, and to send them to the director of the research unit. Some pscyhologists have thought that we should at the very outset have started with a questionnaire. With this I disagree. Quite apart from the likelihood that many might be put off by such an approach, the very manner of asking the questions would be apt, I believe, to give a slant to the contents of the replies. The specimens we are hunting are shy and delicate ones which we want to secure in as natural a condition as possible. We must at all costs avoid damaging or distorting them by trying to trap them within an artificial framework. In the first instance we want a brief description set down in the words and manner thought most fitting by those who have had the experience. Later on those working on particular types of experience have indeed used the questionnaire method for eliciting further information about the different kinds of experience.

This first part of our investigation was aimed at giving us a general idea of the many different kinds of experience that may be present in the population. It is the observational foundation which, as in biology, precedes the quantitative studies of the science of ecology. The naturalists are the pioneers describing the nature of what will later be treated in a more systematic fashion, as we shall come to see presently (p. 224).

How was our large collection of material to be catalogued? At first, with my biological background, I had thought that we might classify the records with a system not unlike that used by the naturalists. Perhaps to begin with we would divide them into two main kinds (almost like the division between the plant and animal kingdoms), with on the one hand those describing a general sense of spiritual awareness and on the other those which were of a more dramatic, ecstatic or mystic character. Then I had imagined that the various individual examples within each of these main divisions could be classed in hierarchical systems like biological specimens; those of the same kind might form a labelled unit corresponding to a species, and such units whose members were all slightly different from those of other units yet had many points in common could be grouped together into a higher category, and these into yet higher ones, and so on. We very soon found, however, that such a system could not work, for the whole situation was much more complex.

Very few of the accounts of experience can be put *as a*

whole into just one particular classificatory compartment. So many of them were a mixture of widely different items. Indeed some of them combined together features characteristic of the two main classes into which I had first thought to divide them. For example, a person who for long had been either an agnostic or an atheist might suddenly have an entirely unexpected ecstatic or mystical type of experience and then, having come to feel that the universe was not at all the sort of place he had imagined it to be, he began to develop a general sense of spiritual awareness. It soon became evident that our system must be one of distinguishing all the different elements which in varying combinations were to make up the different experiences rather than one attempting to classify the whole individual accounts themselves, of which hardly any two offered exactly the same set of ingredients.

We drew up a list of twelve main divisions, each of which was subdivided to give a number of subsidiary categories. It must always be remembered that we are studying and classifying the *written* accounts of such experiences, which are as near as we can get to the subjective feelings themselves. The initial statements, however, may be supplemented by further statements, elicited as I have already said by further questioning, to bring us nearer to the actual nature of the experience than did the original record. The broad outline of the classification was first made by Timothy Beardsworth, our philosophical colleague, and then added to and modified in discussions at various staff meetings.[1] The twelve main divisions are given numbers and each of these is divided into a varying number of smaller subdivisions distinguished by letters (a), (b), (c), (d), etc. so that each particular experience can then be given a descriptive label which will indicate its nature to any future student of the material. Some may just have only one character, say 1(c) or 7(b); or, as is more usual, have several components to be distinguished, for example, as 1(d), 7(e), or 6(a), 7(a), 8(c), to cite but two of the hundreds

[1] Regarding staff see section on Acknowledgement (on p. 9).

of possible combinations. Such classificatory labels are briefly informative, just as in chemistry the formula H_2SO_4 tells us the different elements involved in the composition of sulphuric acid. In mentioning such an analogy I hope it will not be thought that we regard the experiences as made up in any such way as is a chemical compound; they merely indicate a similar method of labelling. Any experience is of course not just the adding together of a number of different components; it is very much a case of the whole being greater than the sum of the parts.

As promised to the writers, each individual record is treated as strictly confidential; all names and addresses of persons, or names of places which might reveal their identity, are eliminated in any extracts being published or made available to *bona-fide* students working on such experiences. Each account is given a serial number and all the original letters are kept locked up in fire-proof cabinets; typed extracts, however, from all the accounts giving the essential parts are then available in files under their reference numbers for those wishing to work on them.

The material is very uneven, both in quantity and quality, which makes any detailed quantitative study of it impossible, except merely to indicate the relative numerical frequency of the different types. This stage, as I have emphasized, is one essentially of natural history and not of a quantitative science like ecology; the statistical treatment will, as I have said, come later in the investigations using random samples. Qualitatively it is also heterogeneous; variations in educational and cultural background mean that whilst in some accounts there is no difficulty in understanding the delicate differences in the writer's feelings, in others it is extremely hard to know how much one may legitimately read into a description which may be largely inarticulate or incoherent but which nevertheless does indicate some genuine and deeply felt experience.

In spite of these difficulties the main object of the first part of the research has been achieved in giving us a knowledge of the many different kinds of experience that may be met with among those members of the public who are willing to give an expression of them. My last book *The Spiritual Nature of Man* (Oxford University Press, 1979) is based upon a study of the first 3,000 such accounts, and in it will be found examples of all the different categories in our classification;[2] here I am only concerned to give a general idea of the evidence available as illustrated by just a selection of examples taken from only a limited number of categories.

I will first outline the nature of the twelve main divisions of the classification. The first four are all in the field of what we may call sensory or quasi-sensory experiences: 1 visual, 2 auditory, 3 touch and 4 (rare) smell. Then follow as 5 the experiences we classify as supposed extra-sensory perception, 6 the behavioural changes, and 7 the cognitive or affective elements. Next, under 8, the development of experiences, we classify all the different ways in which the writers' religious feelings arose and expanded with the course of time, and followed, under 9, by the dynamic patterns of experience, and under 10 dream experiences. Then we have 11, the antecedents or 'triggers' of experience in which the writers give accounts of the many different factors that have given rise to their state of spiritual awareness, and finally 12, the records describing the effects which these experiences may have had on the lives of those concerned.

It will only be possible in one chapter to make a general review of some of the different kinds of experience and to record their relative frequency. Some readers may be surprised at my including what we have called the sensory or quasi-sensory experiences along with other kinds which most would regard as of a more deeply spiritual nature; however, we shall see that some can indeed have such significance. I take two examples, one each from the two sub-categories of our main division 1 – visual experiences. The first concerns the sensation of light. It is one of a great many recording

[2] The Oxford University Press has now published a paperback edition which I hope will be available to students in schools and universities.

similar impressions. Two undergraduates had been having a tense discussion on the nature of life and the writer describes her experience as follows:

> In between her question and the uncontrollable tears which started to filter down my face, was a timeless moment. Then I experienced great fear; something invisible, yet momentous, was happening in the room . . . [which] all of a sudden seemed to be filled with light, a whitish, yet warm, light. It seemed to be both in the room and within me. Although 'it' was obviously outside me, it was also part of me; yet a part with no physical location. It was united completely with a region of my mind. The curious thing is that I *felt* the light. Although my eyes were open, the perception of the light was an interior perception. I continued to see everything in the room quite clearly, but all the objects were lit up by this interior light.
>
> As soon as I perceived this light, I felt great joy and peace; I wanted to worship the force which was manifesting itself in such an inexpressible way and which had come to comfort us in answer to our searching. I cannot say how long this state lasted. (1519)

My second example comes from the sub-category of visions. Such experiences are more common than many people suppose. Among our first three thousand records received there were no fewer than 544 examples sent in by those who felt them to be of a religious nature. Professor H. H. Price, when Wykeham Professor of Logic at Oxford, wrote a preface to Tyrrell's book *Apparitions* (1943) in which he sums up the situation as follows:

> The tea-party question, 'Do you believe in ghosts?' is one of the most ambiguous which can be asked. But if we take it to mean, 'Do you believe that people sometimes experience apparitions?' the answer is that they certainly do. No one who examines the evidence can

come to any other conclusion. Instead of disputing the facts, we must try to explain them. But whatever explanation we offer, we soon find ourselves in very deep waters indeed.

It is well known among psychologists that, with suitable subjects, apparitions can be produced at will by an experimenter using hypnotic suggestion. Under such conditions the subject may see and describe Mr A. coming into the room, when it is entirely imaginary, or he may be made to fondle a kitten on his knee, describing it, stroking it, and so on. It seems likely that such visions may well be reproduced among normal people at moments of particular emotional stress. I give the following example:

> I decided to go away from those who could bring pressure to bear and for a week stayed with an elderly and wise friend in the Lake District. My question was whether or not I should be confirmed and so become an Anglican. Every day throughout the week I prayed and thought. My major prayer was 'Dear Lord, what do you want me to do?' It was a week of coldness and darkness with no indication of any kind – UNTIL on the evening before I was due to return to London I spent several hours by myself sitting on a sofa. I was unaware of time. I then saw with great vividness the FEET OF OUR LORD some twelve feet from the floor and with that vision was the overwhelming thought of ORDINATION, which hitherto had never entered my head.
>
> That was the answer to my prayer and in consequence I was ordained . . . The clarity of this 'vision' was to me unmistakable and I owe my vocation to it . . .
>
> To me there is no doubt about the validity of this spiritual experience and the turning-point and signpost that it was. (2166)

Now let me pass to our second main division, that of auditory experiences. The hearing of voices is only a little less frequent than seeing visions, and at times both visions and voices may be seen and heard together. Among the first three thousand experiences, 431 described such voices. The phenomenon is by no means confined to those who are religious; I have in an earlier book recalled what Bernard Shaw wrote in his preface to his play *Saint Joan*. It is worth repeating. Having pointed out that our criminal lunatic asylums contain many whose acts of homicide have been committed in obedience to voices they claim to have heard, this does not lead him to dismiss the maid's voices as irrelevant, as we see in the following quotation from the same preface (p. xiv):

> Joan's voices and visions have played many tricks with her reputation. They have been held to prove that she was mad, that she was a liar and imposter, that she was a sorceress (she was burned for this), and finally that she was a saint. They do not prove any of these things; but the variety of the conclusions reached show how little our matter-of-fact historians know about other people's minds, or even about their own. There are people in the world whose imagination is so vivid that when they have an idea it comes to them as an audible voice, sometimes uttered by a visible figure.

Socrates, Saint Francis, Saint Joan, Luther, Swedenborg, and Blake are prominent examples from history of those whose vivid religious imagination caused them to see visions and hear voices; in our own day we have had the striking testimony of both in the remarkable life of the founder of the Burrswood centre for spiritual healing, the late Miss Dorothy Kerin, in *The Living Touch* (1914) and *Fulfilling* (1960). Whatever the psychological cause for such phenomena, there can be no doubt that they often make a most profound impression upon those who experience them, and their religious significance may be great.

I will give just one example of the hearing of a voice from our collection. It is as follows:

But the great experience that led me to be ordained was when I was about 17 . . . I went on a lonely walking tour with a sheepdog on the Whitby and Scarborough Moors which have a wonderful and spiritual atmosphere . . . It was towards the end of this tour that one morning I was drawing near the ruins of Rievaulx Abbey . . . and I sensed a wonderful atmosphere of quiet peace, and then heard a most entrancing voice which in one way seemed external and yet in another from deep down within me, calling me to be ordained. I saw nothing, yet I was convinced it was Christ himself and he desired me like Andrew and Peter to rise up and follow him and be ordained. With the voice came the inner conviction that Christ would make all things possible. (711).

From division 5 – supposed extra-sensory perception – I take just one example from the sub-category 5(a) telepathy. Many scientists will still not accept at its face value the evidence that has been put forward for what has been called telepathy: the supposed communication between one mind and another by means other than those of the physical sense organs. The reasons for this reluctance I have discussed at length elsewhere and we need not go into them here. I have also in these books expressed my doubts as to whether the well known card-guessing experiments (the results of which can, I believe, no longer be denied) are really demonstrating telepathy, but are in fact revealing something very different yet no less remarkable about the nature of our universe. This latter view is discussed in a book of joint authorship by Hardy, Harvie and Koestler, *The Challenge of Chance* (Hutchinson, 1973).

The follow is the example I take:

One of these incidents concerned a married friend who had problems which had brought him to a point nearing breakdown. During a telephone conversation he spoke suddenly of his distress and misery and I longed to help him. Hugh thought that if I could give any comfort I

215

should go to see him but I was quite certain that, as a married woman, this was something I could not do in the present circumstances and instead I went on my knees saying, 'I know I may not go to him, but if I could go, this is what I'd say' – and I said to God all that was in my heart to give comfort to our friend.

Some days later I met him unexpectedly and he said, 'I'm feeling better. If you ever get as low as that, remember this', and he proceeded to tell me, almost word for word, what I said on my knees. I have no doubt that we had met on some different plane and God has used me to bring him the comfort it would have been entirely wrong to give in any other way. (2023)

I will give two very different examples from our division 6 which deals with behavioural changes. The first is from sub-category (b) – healing – and is only one excerpt from a very long account sent in by a clergyman:

Eventually, after months of reluctance – for I am by nature a sceptic! or more accurately want to know why and how and I am indeed sceptical of sudden emotional decisions and overwhelming spiritual certainties – I was pushed into the practice of the ministry of healing. It was not another human being that pushed me; I was merely faced by a situation in which I could only do one of two things, either show a visitor the door, regretfully declining to do as asked, lay my hands on the person in the name of Jesus, or do just that. I chose the second course. For some years after this, I kept a strict record of every person with whom I had more than a passing contact; in other words, I kept notes on what happened to the whole person to whom I ministered . . .

I do not look upon myself as, like Time, the Great Healer, but with a certain shyness and humility – more than that, with a grateful certainty that it is not I who heal, but a power outside me, using me as an instrument – I have called again and again on this power that makes for and wills righteousness . . . (270)

My second example from this division comes under 6(d) – heroism – under which we have very few records, perhaps because natural modesty prevents many from describing their own heroic actions. This is the one I have chosen:

The clearest and greatest example of this awareness of what I believe was the presence of God came to me during the night of 7 August 1915 – the landing of thousands of troops at Sulva Bay. Under fire for the first time was very trying, and at first I was afraid as most men were. As man after man went down, however, a presence came to me which took away all my fears and replaced them with a feeling of ecstasy. Everything was overwhelmed with this feeling and I was for the time a brave man, without a fear or anxiety in the world. During that night I was severely wounded and disabled in consequence . . . The memory of this night however and the few other occasions when I have been favoured with this nearness of God, have been the outstanding experiences of my long life . . . (15)

We now come to the largest division of our classification, number 7, that concerned with cognitive and affective elements. These cover a very wide field and we have had to divide them into as many as twenty-two sub-categories. These experiences cover all those feelings which are most generally associated with the spiritual side of man: the sense of joy, peace, security, awe, reverence and wonder; also there are feelings of exaltation and ecstasy, of harmony and unity, of hope and fulfilment; then again the sense of timelessness, the sense of purpose, and the sense of prayer answered in events. There are also experiences of the darker side: feelings of remorse and guilt, of fear and horror.

I had at first thought that the cognitive side – the learning something from an experience – should be separated from the emotional elements associated with or resulting from it. In practice, however, any such distinction breaks down; therefore in this main division we have both the cognitive and affective elements mixed up together, whereas they should perhaps come under even more sub-categories than I have used, but that would have made classification much too unwieldly. The first sub-category, 7(a), deals with the sense of security, protection and peace. We received no fewer than 759 accounts from the first three thousand records. I will take just one example:

> In 1939 . . . I was appointed to a post I had always wanted . . . but in 1945 I had to resign for personal reasons . . . This was a great disappointment and I had no idea what else I should do . . . After wrestling with this problem for some weeks, I was sitting one summer afternoon under a weeping willow tree in a Cambridge garden. Time seemed to stand still. The quiet seclusion calmed the turmoil in my mind; I was able to stand back from it and clearly place the whole situation before God committing the future entirely to him. Plans took shape and seemed entirely right and appropriate and with them was given the confidence that I should be helped through any difficulties that might arise. The peace and strength and support from this encounter has never left me and has slowly grown as other opportunities have developed. (522)

7(b) is the sense of joy, happiness and well-being. Extraordinary ecstatic feelings of joy may be experienced under the most unlikely conditions and they may often lead to a profound realization of the spiritual side of life, yet they by no means always do so. The student of the subject must take very seriously the careful studies of Marghanita Laski in her book *Ecstasy: a Study of some Secular and Religious Experiences* (1961); here she applies the systematic, almost ecological method to compare the records of subjective feelings experienced by memebrs of three different groups of people.

218

Although she calls herself an atheist and is certainly as much opposed to any concept of God as a human-like figure 'out there' as she is to institutional religion, I cannot help feeling that she is not as anti-religious as most people (perhaps indeed including herself) imagine.

One of the most interesting accounts of extraordinary ecstatic experience in our collection is the following:

I could not call myself a mystic, but on half-a-dozen occasions I have had experiences which *for me* made me certain of the reality of some supernatural entity which, or whom, I label 'God' . . .

It would be boring to describe them all, but they all had similar characteristics. I will try to describe one. Vauxhall Station on a murky November Saturday evening is not the setting one would choose for a revelation of God! I was a young theological student aged nineteen, being sent from Richmond Theological College (London University) to take the services somewhere . . .

But the great moment came and when, years later, I read C. S. Lewis's *Surprised by Joy* I thought, 'Yes, I know exactly how he felt. I felt like that.' For a few seconds only, I suppose, the whole compartment was filled with light. This is the only way I know in which to describe the moment, for there was nothing to *see* at all. I felt caught up into some tremendous sense of being within a loving, triumphant and shining purpose. I never felt more humble. I never felt more exalted. A most curious, but overwhelming sense possessed me and filled me with ecstasy. I felt that all was well for mankind – how poor the words seem! The word 'well' is so poverty-stricken. All men were shining and glorious beings who in the end would enter incredible joy. Beauty, music, joy, love immeasurable and a glory unspeakable, all this they would inherit. Of this they were heirs. My puny message, if I passed my exams and qualified as a minister, would contribute only an infinitesimal drop to the ocean of love and truth which God wanted men to enjoy . . .

All this happened over fifty years ago but even now I can see myself in the corner of that dingy, third-class compartment with the feeble lights of inverted gas mantles overhead and the Vauxhall Station platform outside with milk cans standing there. In a few moments the glory departed – all but one curious, lingering feeling. I loved everybody in that compartment. It sounds silly now, and indeed I blush to write it, but at that moment I think I would have died for any one of the people in that compartment . . . (385)

In contrast to this full and dramatic account I give one of a much more humble nature which nevertheless has a striking quality of its own:

At 17 I was confused and questing, nothing made a lot of sense, the world seemed so unfair and people unreliable. However, I had not forgotten how to pray, and I prayed with unashamed sincerity that if God existed could he show me some sort of light in the jungle.

One day I was sweeping the stairs down in the house in which I was working, when suddenly I was overcome, overwhelmed, saturated, no word is adequate, with a sense of most sublime and living *LOVE*. It not only affected me, but seemed to bring everything around me to *LIFE*. The brush in my hand, my dustpan, the stairs, seemed to come alive with part of this infinite power of love, so utterly and overwhelmingly wonderful that one knew at once what the saints had grasped. It could only have been a minute or two, yet for that brief particle of time it seemed eternity. Why I should have been so privileged I will never know. But I think my prayers were answered by being taught that one purpose of our lives is simply to learn to love. (1753)

7(i) is the sense of harmony, order, unity. The experiences in this section have no quasi-sensory element in them, which distinguishes them from those placed in sub-section 1(d) where people felt at unity with their surroundings in a visual sense. I give just one example from the 200 accounts we possess of this sense of unity:

> About 1962 I spent four hours standing at a busy road centre in Birmingham (a city I hardly knew) with five or six others in a peace vigil. At the three previous vigils in which I had taken part, I felt cut off from – perhaps a little superior to – the general public hurrying past, and had spent much of my time trying to pray for them, for those at war and for world peace. On this occasion I found instead that I was overtaken by an intense feeling of affection for and unity with everyone around as they ran to catch buses, took children shopping or joyfully met their friends. The feeling was so strong that I wanted to leave my silent vigil and join them in their urgent living.
>
> This sense of 'oneness' is basic to what I understand of religion. Hitherto I think I had only experienced it so irresistibly towards a few individuals, sometimes towards my children, or when in love.
>
> The effect of the experience has been, I think, a permanent increase in my awareness that we are 'members one of another', a consequent greater openness towards all and a widening of my concern for others. (504)

7(u) is the sense of prayer answered in events. I give one example of each of two kinds of events considered to be the result of prayer (415 accounts were sent in). The first illustrates changes in the person's sense of well-being and mental balance, whereas the second deals with what at first sight seems to be the more mundane matter of raising funds, yet the real issue, of course is – in the words of the account – 'our *ability* to raise the money' (italics mine). In both there is a new power generated from the process of devout prayer.

Crying out in despair one night, praying as I have never prayed before or since, utterly dejected and miserable, a condition brought upon myself by my own stupid folly and woeful ignorance; nevertheless, developments showed quite plainly that prayer was answered. From that time forward I felt new power; an inexpressible joy flowed through my whole being, and a certain sense of forgiveness anew. Mental balance restored, I became aware of moral obligation, and the urge to start life afresh. (135)

At last, after six years of pressure, the West C— Hospital Management Committee invited us to provide the necessary money to erect a centre at T— Hospital in conjunction with the physiotherapy department which would be run by them for observation and treatment of our spastic and disabled children. Some of us regarded this as an impossibility; I reminded them that Jesus Christ said 'Whatever you ask, in prayer, believing, you shall receive.' For I never doubted our ability to raise the money. So now it is available and early next year the centre will be erected at a cost of £22,000. All these things have been accomplished in a miraculous manner. (373)

Turning now to our category 8, concerned with the development of experience: the gradual growth of a sense of awareness or a more or less continuous experience. Here I will give three examples, and no comment is needed, for they speak for themselves.

All my life seems to have been a gradual unfolding of understanding, a slow development. Only in the last year or two has this seemed to reach religious experience . . . I now feel purpose in life. I must become 'better'. From time to time I realize I am becoming slightly more aware. This immense drive I feel pushing me to deepen my knowledge of self – this I know to reach towards the whole meaning of the universe. (820)

There has been a growing sense of personal encounter with a power, at the same time within and outside me, that has never left me since the original relationship began. However much I betray the relationship in feeling, thought and action, it remains with me. I no longer think of God in the anthropomorphic sense that I used to do . . . It is as if some power quite beyond my understanding has been doing continuous sorting of spiritual luggage, leaving me with the few basic certainties and helping me to travel light so far as theological problems are concerned. (144)

As I look back it seems that my whole life has been a religious experience, in the sense that my religious consciousness has grown and developed as inevitably as my body and mind. (238)

We come now to our main division 9: dynamic patterns in experience. I will give just two examples:

I have found prayer always helps; provided I am honest with God and ask for help in the right way – not to get out of a mess I don't like, but to be given help and strength to go through with it. My greatest insights about myself have come when I have prayed. I have been so impressed by the immense patience God seems to show. I may desert him for years, but whenever I turn back, he always seems to be there, waiting. I think prayer is a question of leaving oneself open to any answer that may come – very often unexpected and not what one wanted, and yet it always leaves me with awe, reverence and gladness that I have made the effort. This seems to be a point: we have to make the initial effort. We are then met more than half way, but he never intrudes on us. He waits for us to approach him. (111)

In our efforts to know the power we call God, it is only too evident to me that the desire and *the initiative MUST come from the individual himself*. Always prayer will be from the bottom of the heart, and always offered in the certainty that the answer or the power or the event will be forthcoming – when the time is ripe and not until. However, it has been my experience that *the answer will not be made available to us unless we have first prepared the way to the utmost of our ability at the time*. (261)

I will not here deal with the last three main divisions 10, 11 and 12. 10 is concerned with dream experiences, which I feel are not at all of the same value of evidence as the experiences recorded in the other categories. 11 is concerned with the antecedents or 'triggers' which the correspondents feel led up to their particular experience and are not in the same way setting out the actual events, although they are interesting enough, showing how experiences may be produced by music, visual art, literature, drama, etc. The last main category is concerned with the consequences of the experiences. Here again we are not so much concerned with the actual nature of the experiences themselves, but are dealing with the effects they have had on people's lives.

Whilst our natural history survey has told us much about the kinds of experience which may occur among 3,000 members of the general public it cannot provide us with any idea of the proportions in a population who may feel this or that experience or indeed none at all. This can only be done by random sampling methods which were set out as the third stage in our proposed research programme in the lecture I gave to The Royal Institution in 1969.[3] In the meantime, however, Mr David Hay, Lecturer in Biology in the Department of Education at the University of Nottingham, to whom I have already referred (p. 189) had quite independently developed a keen interest in a similar line of research

[3] A Scientist Looks at Religion, *Proceedings of The Royal Institution of Great Britain*, vol. 43, no. 201, London.

and had begun a pilot survey among his students in preparation for a larger venture; I was delighted when he wrote expressing the hope that his work might be done in co-operation with ours, and we were able to appoint as a member of our staff a sociologist to work with him in Nottingham (see p. 9). They carried out two pieces of research which although differing in methods were essentially complementary. One included questions in one of the regular nation-wide surveys conducted by National Opinion Polls Limited, which yielded a total of 1865 people (853 male and 1012 female) who responded to the questions on religious experience; the other was a more intimate survey, on the lines of the original pilot study, made in depth by tactful interviews among randomly selected members of the general public in the Nottingham area.

In addition to comparing their findings with those of a number of similar surveys in the USA they present some very interesting results which I can only briefly touch on. They consider two suggestions that have been made in the past by some psychologists and anthropologists: that religious experience is more often reported among those who are oppressed by an unjust society in that it might have a palliative function, or that it is associated with a low level of psychological well-being. If the first proposition were true one would expect to find a higher proportion of those who give a positive response to the key question among the lower social classes than among the upper strata; in fact the results of their survey are quite contrary to this. Nor does the nation-wide survey give support to the hypothesis that religious experience is associated with a low level of psychological well-being or neurosis, for in it they included the Bradburn Balanced Affect Scale (Bradburn 1969) as a short measure of psychological well-being. The range of possible scores on the scale is from minus 5, indicating a very low level of psychological well-being, to plus 5, indicating a very high level. Approximately equal sized high and low scoring groups were formed by splitting the sample at the $+1/+2$ scoring boundary. They show that people reporting religious experience are significantly more likely to report a high level of psychological well-being than those who do not.

At the end of Chapter 10 I gave an extract from one of three short talks David Hay gave in the BBC's 'Thought for the Day' series; I will now quote from another of those talks in which in his own words he gives some of his thoughts about his important work. He begins thus:

> I wonder if you have ever been alone, perhaps at a time of deep distress in your life, or its opposite, when you have been very happy and had an experience like this:
>
> At a certain point, although you can see or hear nothing, to your surprise you become aware that you are not alone; that you are surrounded by what can only be called a powerful and protective presence. Along with the presence there is usually a feeling of reassurance and peace which sometimes turns into ecstatic delight, and you may find yourself deeply moved, to the point of tears.
>
> On the basis of at least ten large-scale surveys carried out in this country and the United States over the past fifteen years or so, we now know that well over a third of the adult population of the two countries would claim to have had an experience like this at least once in their lives. For Britain, that means about fifteen million people. Recently I've been directing an indepth study of these experiences among a random sample of the adult population of Nottingham. In the safer environment of a lengthy private interview, over 60% felt able to admit they'd had this kind of awareness. Usually they gave it a religious interpretation, even though many of them seldom or never went to church.
>
> Most people felt grateful for their experience and that their lives had been changed for the better. It seemed to give them a sense of solidarity with their fellow human beings and with the natural world around them. They

felt as if they belonged. If they were irreligious before their experience, it often made them more tolerant towards religion. Believers felt they'd had practical confirmation of their beliefs and were more inclined to act in accordance with the moral teachings of their faith.

All the research both here and in America tells a similar story. People reporting these experiences, when compared with others, are *more* likely to be personally happy, find life meaningful, be psychologically balanced and open, and socially responsible, and *less* likely to be materialistic, racist or authoritarian in outlook. At the same time, they are usually extraordinarily shy about mentioning their experience to anyone. This is so strong that it amounts to a taboo; several of those we interviewed had never told anyone else at all about their experience, even – or especially – when it meant a great deal to them. When questioned about this taboo, people said they feared that they would be ridiculed for being stupid, or thought to be mentally unbalanced. This is in spite of the fact that on average as a group they appear to be, if anything, more competent and sane than other people.

I have a feeling that this discrepancy has something to do with the very bad image that religion has acquired amongst the dominant intellectual establishment in Europe during the past two to three hundred years . . .

The purpose of this chapter has been to give only an indication of the kinds of experiences we have been studying at the Oxford Unit and in collaboration with David Hay's religious experience research project at Nottingham. If you study the fuller accounts given in my book *The Spiritual Nature of Man*, and consider them together with the material discussed in Chapters 10 and 11, I think you must come to agree that, whatever may be the cause, here is something very deep and real in human nature and that it cannot all be attributed to superstition or childish wishful thinking; these latter ingredients are no doubt mixed in with a number of records, but they are certainly not the whole element in the vast majority of examples. I believe that parallel studies will come to be made in regard to peoples of many different faiths, as William James recommended in his introduction to Starbuck's *Psychology of Religion* which I quoted on p. 193.

I am convinced that these observing naturalists, by confirming, in our scientific age, the teachings of the sages of the past, are going to give us as new an outlook on the nature of man, and indeed of life itself, as did the great field naturalists who gave us the convincing evidence for the reality of evolution in the last century. We must see how it may be possible for these two fundamental elements to be combined. My next and final chapter is an essay which attempts to suggest how such a reconciliation might be brought about.

13

Darwinism with a Difference

What an extraordinary position it is that the intellectual world is now finding itself to be in. A large section of the public, including some of the best brains, has been convinced by the work of the molecular biologists that the neo-Darwinian doctrine of today is pointing only to a materialistic interpretation of life. I have already indicated that I am myself an ardent neo-Darwinian, but I must also admit that all my life I have been one of those who has had a sense of spiritual awareness. Just what I mean by this I shall explain in subsequent pages. How difficult it is to see how this so-called spiritual element in man can be a part of the system of evolution, yet I believe it must be so.

The purpose of this final chapter is twofold. Firstly to suggest, with all humility, how the Darwinian doctrine might be altered – or added to is perhaps a better expression – to bring about a reconciliation between the two outlooks; it is better, I believe, to suggest something which may lead to a discussion of the subject, than to remain silent as if no solution can be found to so difficult a problem. Some of my colleagues would say that I should content myself with 'the art of the soluble'; for me, however, speculation is the fuel of intellectual progress, *provided* that one makes every effort to test one's ideas by observation or experiment. Today it happens to be the fashion in biology to look upon speculation as an irresponsibility, whereas in cosmology one can venture into the possible explanations of black holes, pulsars and other phenomena without any eyebrows being raised. Secondly my purpose is to say a little more about what I myself mean when I speak of the spiritual side of man or indeed when I refer to a power that *appears* as if it were beyond the self, and which we may refer to as God.

Let me first deal with the evolutionary problem. I am sure there can be no doubt that the bodies of animals and man are exceedingly complicated machines, and that all their movement and reactions can be described in physical and chemical terms. Their heredity too is transmitted by a material system – a plan drawn up (by the action of selection) in the chemical code of the DNA. As far as we know, but we must not be dogmatically certain, the whole of the plant kingdom with all its amazing and complex adaptations would appear to be an entirely mechanistic physico-chemical system evolved by the same kind of interplay between the 'architectural' plan of the DNA and Darwinian natural selection as the incorporating or rejecting agent. At first sight it appears to be exactly the same mechanism as that of animal evolution; where then is the difference? If the evolution of plants is entirely a materialistic system, why not also that of animals and man? Who has not been amazed at first seeing a highly speeded up film of a climbing plant growing up some trellis and throwing its tendrils upwards and over some supporting structure just like a monkey throwing its arms round the branches of a tree? Or who has not seen the sticky leaves of the sundew (*Drosera*) catch a fly, first by the fly sticking to its surface, and then with the tentacle-like structures that cover its surface bending over to clutch it just like the tentacles of a polyp enclosing some unfortunate prey. Certainly such comparisons between the evolution of animals and plants must make one realize that the vast majority of animal adaptations must be brought about in a similar automatic way as those of plants. I deliberately want to drive this home but at the same time to point out a crucial difference. The higher animals at least, if not the lower ones, are, as pointed out in Chapter 8, conscious beings; consciousness would appear to be the key to this difference.

Biologists will usually say that the fundamental difference

between animals and plants is not a matter of their locomotive power, for there are many microscopic plants which can swim through the water, it is concerned with their mode of feeding. Plants alone are able to build up their bodies from inorganic chemicals, such as oxygen, hydrogen, carbon, phosphates and nitrates, using the energy of sunlight in the remarkable process of photosynthesis to build up simple organic substances. They split up the molecules of carbon-dioxide, liberate the oxygen, and combine the carbon with the oxygen and hydrogen of water to form simple carbohydrates, which are then elaborated into more complex components by being combined with various minerals in solution. Animals cannot do this; they must have what we call organic food: proteins, carbohydrates (sugars, starch and the like) and fats which have already been built up in the bodies of other animals or of plants. The possibility of consciousness being a cardinal difference between animals and plants is never mentioned, to talk of consciousness in biology has been taboo; it is so because no explanation in terms of physics or chemistry has been found for it.

There is a very fundamental fact about the nature of life upon which perhaps I should have commented before this. Physically life is maintained as a continuing chemical reaction which we call metabolism. It is a dual process – a building up and a breaking down; by the taking in of food and assimilating it, the body is built up into its various constituent tissues and then by a burning-like oxidation process within the tissues themselves the driving energy of our machine is supplied, particularly that of muscular movement. In the young the building up is the stronger and we witness growth, during the greater part of our life the two activities are balanced, but then the building up declines and we can no longer keep pace with the wearing out; we see the onset of old age leading eventually to death. My reason for recalling this here is to make those who may not have thought of it before realize what a remarkable process life is on its physical side. I remember with what awe I was struck as a schoolboy when first I realized that my own metabolism – the system that kept me alive – was actually a continuation of the *very same* chemical reaction that was set going some thousands of millions of years ago. In chemistry I had produced reactions in a test-tube, but here was one that was capable of going on for ever; it is handed on in the unspecialized germ cells, as we saw in fig. 11 (p. 89) and is potentially immortal.

All the views I am now going to put forward are entirely personal ones; I must not arrogantly suppose that they are true. They are but suggestions towards a solution of this, perhaps the greatest of all problems – suggestions to stimulate discussion.

I have already indicated that an animal's power of choice – conscious choice I believe – can act by behavioural selection within the Darwinian system. The various organs of the body, like the hands and feet, I have said, whilst fully described in terms of physics and chemistry, have been selected to a larger and larger degree among the higher animals by the conscious behaviour of the animals themselves. I have always proclaimed that I am not a vitalist in the old fashioned sense of supposing that there is some mystical element operating within the material mechanism of the body; nevertheless, if I am to be honest, I must admit that I am a vitalist of a special kind. I suppose that my position is not far from that most unfashionable Bergsonian theory of creative evolution, but with the most important proviso that I am also a Darwinian. Bergson, as did Teilhard de Chardin, failed to appreciate the real nature of the Darwinian doctrine; and because of this his biological philosophy is never considered today. I would like to see it revived in a new form. I have always looked with contempt at the supposed witty gibe against Bergson that we might just as well speak of an *élan locomotif* to describe the working of a railway engine as to speak, as he did, of an *élan vital* as an explanation of life; the engine, of course, is a particular form of tool – an extension of man's own locomotive power – invented by the very impulse of which Bergson speaks in his more poetic language.

How am I to link this conscious behaviour, which works within the Darwinian system by means of its particular form of selection, to the subsequent development of religion and the spiritual nature of man? I must make another admission. In company with some of the more philosophical biologists such as Sir Charles Sherrington, Sir John Eccles, Sir Cyril Hinshelwood and philosophers such as A. N. Whitehead and Sir Karl Popper, I must admit to being a dualist, i.e. one who believes that the universe has at least a double nature,[1] being not entirely material, but having an equally important mental and spiritual element. Sherrington, nearing the end of his life, wrote in his introduction to a new edition of his famous work *The Integrative Action of the Nervous System* (Cambridge University Press, 1947) 'that our being should consist of *two* fundamental elements offers I suppose no greater inherent improbability than that it should rest on only one'. You may remember that I have quoted other relevant statements by Sherrington on p. 159.

If we are attempting to link man's spiritual nature with evolution, are we to suppose that animals may have some form of experience coming from somewhere other than through their organs of sense? It would appear to be most unlikely, and anyway we could never know. However, when the change came in evolution, as discussed in Chapter 9, we can see that primitive man, with his new powers of communication by language and the handing on of tradition as a result of shared experience could develop feelings of a new awareness. They could build up a general tradition of there being some element with which they could make contact; and if they approached it with a certain reverence, with a devotional feeling, with in fact a form of love akin to that between child and parent, they would in return feel a lifting

[1] I say 'at least' a double nature because there are some, such as Sir John Eccles and Sir Karl Popper, who believe that one should distinguish three such elements; this, however, I must not go into here.

up of the self, a new sense of confidence, a power to overcome difficulties, a force to make them stronger, a something that gave more courage than they had ever had before. They might call it *mana*, *waken*, *nhialic*, *knoth*, and other names; and later it could be called God. We can in fact see its link with evolution; it would have, in the words of Marett, 'survival value' in that those primitive tribes which developed more courage, felt themselves receiving this support, would more likely be successful in the struggle for life.

There is another way in which I believe, and it is of course only speculative, that man's religious side may be linked with evolution; it is an idea which I put forward in *The Divine Flame* (1966) and then more fully in *The Biology of God* (1975). Before explaining it I should, however, make clear that I do not believe in God as a kind of old gentleman out there; that image, as Bishop John Robinson said in his *Honest to God* (1963) must go. Nevertheless I am sure that our relationship with what we call God must be a personal one; it must be an intimate I – Thou relationship – in fact a deep love relationship. In the world of living things there are two different deeply felt kinds of love; that between the sexes and that between offspring and parents; that between man and that spiritual element he calls God is of the latter kind. The first of the two great commandments for a Christian is that 'Thou shalt love thy God with all thy heart'; and God is presented to us as a parent: 'Our Father which art in Heaven'. Now there is a curious parallel between this love of God and something which has occurred within the animal world as I must now explain; it concerns the relationship between a dog and man.

There are various theories as to the way the dog became attached to man, but we need not be concerned with which may be the correct one; once attached, however, the dog underwent a curious change. The idea of what I am going to suggest came to me after reading that great pioneer of the study of animal behaviour, Konrad Lorenz, in his book *King Solomon's Ring*. Let me quote part of him as follows:

The really single-hearted devotion of a dog to its master has two quite different sources. On the one side, it is nothing else than the submissive attachment which every wild dog shows towards his pack leader, and which is transferred, without any considerable alteration in character, by the domestic dog to a human being. To this is added, in the more highly domesticated dogs, quite another form of affection. Many of the characteristics in which domestic animals differ from their wild ancestral form arise by virtue of the fact that properties of body structure and behaviour, which in the wild prototype are only marked by some transient stages of youth, are kept permanently by the domestic form. In dogs, short hair, curly tail, hanging ears, domed skulls and the short muzzle of many domestic breeds are features of this type. In behaviour, one of these juvenile characters which has become permanent in the domestic dog, expresses itself in the peculiar form of its attachment. The ardent affection which wild canine youngsters show for their mother, and which in these disappears completely after they have reached maturity, is preserved as a permanent mental trait of all highly domesticated dogs. What originally was love for the mother is transformed into love for the human master.

I must not become too biological, but it is worth pointing out that, as Bolk[2] has shown us, man himself displays many youthful characters compared with the earlier primate stock. I need not go into details in support of this, as it is well documented in the biological literature;[3] one such character is our prolonged period of childhood giving greater opportunities for learning and allowing a larger growth of brain by the delayed fusion of the sutures of the skull. It seems to me

[2] L. Bolk, *Das Problem der Menschwerdung*, Jena, 1926.
[3] Well summarized in Sir Gavin de Beer's *Embryos and Ancestors*, Oxford, 1940.

possible that man, who, like the dog, has juvenile characters, e.g. this prolonged period of childhood and a strong child-parent affection, may, also like the dog, have transferred part of the submissiveness which he had shown to his tribal leader, together with his filial affection, to a new master – one of a very unusual kind.

This new master is invisible, yet, as we have seen, has a reality for man all over the world, and is called by many different names and when approached in a particular way – in a very personal, devotional form of prayer – will respond by giving help and encouragement to overcome the difficulties of the world. I hope I shall not be thought to be irreverent – for I mean the very opposite – when I say that I think the nearest thing to the look in the eyes of a dog looking up to his master, is the look in the eyes of someone kneeling at the altar rail. The nature of God remains for us a great mystery; we realize that the conception of a parent-like person is but a childish notion, to help us to have some idea of a much greater truth we cannot yet understand. By experience we (those who are religious) feel help in our lives *as if* from a person; some power for a fuller life comes to us in response to a confidence we place in this strange element when we make an approach *as if* to a person. This is the power that William James speaks of as '*objectively true*' (see p. 199): 'Disregarding the over-beliefs, and confining ourselves to what is common and generic', he says, 'we have in the fact that the conscious person is continuous with a wider self through which saving experiences come, a positive content of religious experience which, it seems to me, is literally and objectively true as far as it goes.' It is the power which, in L. P. Jack's words: 'can help, deliver, illuminate and gladden the soul . . . the companion of the brave . . . the God who is spirit, the God who is love'.

It seems to be likely that the solutions to our individual problems are always within us if only we could reach them, and that the act of prayer brings them to the surface. In *The Divine Flame* (1966, p. 236) I expressed this idea as follows:

Instead of supposing that one great personal-like Deity is thinking out simultaneously the detailed answers to the millions of different problems of all the individuals of the world, is it not more reasonable to suppose that some action is set in motion by prayer which draws the particular solution for each one of us from our own minds? In saying this I must again make clear that I am not implying that I believe this destroys our conception of the divine. All the evidence of religious experience, I believe, shows us that man makes contact with this power which appears partly transcendent, and felt as the numinous beyond the self, and partly immanent within him. I also think it likely, however, that it may well be this uplifting power which does in fact activate the subconscious solution-providing mechanism in a way which would not otherwise be possible. In a similar way it may be the same power which assists in the healing of a sick person.

Such a view I find is not without some theological support; Bishop John Robinson, in his book *Exploration into God* (1967, p. 115) writes as follows:

The God who 'answers' prayers or 'makes' people well again is inevitably seen as disposing the events of nature and history or the lives of individuals in a way which envisages him as standing above the processes, manipulating them from the outside. What we need is a conception of prayer that organically relates the processes themselves to the depths of the divine creativity and love.

I wish now to suggest that the spirituality of man might be increased in the future by what I call an experimental faith. Here I want to use the words *experiment* and *experimental* in a particular way, in fact in their original meaning before they became associated in the modern mind with the methods of science. The first meaning given to the word 'experimental' in the *Concise Oxford Dictionary* is 'Based on experience, not on authority or conjecture'; this being so, would it not be better, some would say, to speak of an experiential faith so as to avoid confusion with the scientific meaning? My answer is 'No', because the faith I am thinking of would be one based not only on general experience but on one which in part is like that described in the first meaning given in the same dictionary to the word 'experiment', i.e. a 'test, trial or procedure adopted on the chance of its succeeding'. 'What a poor kind of faith' the faithful may well say, and I would agree if that were all there is to it; that, however, is not all that I mean. To become a real faith the word 'chance' in the definition must become converted into 'certainty' by the very experiment having succeeded. I do not mean a faith based upon prayer which is undertaken, as it were, just on the off-chance that it may succeed. I mean a prayer undertaken by an agnostic or an atheist who, having studied the records of experience, is now prepared, with profound sincerity, to attempt the quest for a period of, say, at least six months; it might perhaps be a prayer beginning something like this: 'God, if there is a God, help me to find you, and having found you, help me to have the strength and courage to do what I feel to be thy will.' Childish, isn't it? Yes, for that, I believe, is the biological essence of the matter.

The spiritual side of man is not the product of intellectuality. The development of the mind, now so strongly influenced by the achievements of the physical sciences, has tended to dismiss, as childish wishful thinking, this deeper property of life. It is childlike just because it is even more fundamental to life than is this recent amazing innovation of mind; it indeed was the very nature of the teachings of Jesus as they have come down to us: 'Whosoever shall not receive the kingdom of God as a little child, he shall not enter therein.' (Mark 10:15)

When speaking of God as Father, Jesus invariably used the childish word *Abba*. John Taylor, now Bishop of Winchester, in his book *The Go-Between God* (1972), brings out so well the childlike relationship which Jesus had to the presence of God. He writes (on his p. 93) thus:

That . . . trustful dedication points to the dominant I-Thou relationship in this spirit-possessed life, namely his incomparable awareness of God. More than all the others who absorbed his whole attention, this was the other in whom he was immersed. God was the never-forgotten presence, yet Jesus's relation to God was never dutiful; it was ardent and glad and totally relaxed. It expressed the absolute acceptance of his creature-hood and an untroubled dependence, without a shadow of subservience. It was the fully responsible partnership of one who, in Bonhoeffer's phrase, 'made his whole life a response to the question and call of God'. This astonishing relationship was perfectly expressed in the baby-word '*Abba*', 'Daddy', in which we catch the actual sound of Jesus's most characteristic and intimate utterance.

To return to what I was saying about an experimental faith. I like to think that our studies at the Religious Experience Research Unit are not only helping, however modestly, to build up an academic knowledge towards a better understanding of the spiritual nature of man, but that they are, as I have suggested, also providing the evidence which, as it accumulates further in the future, may induce others to make the act of faith which is expressed in the words of Jesus as reported in the Gospels (Mark 7:7 and Luke 11:9): 'Ask and it shall be given you; seek and ye shall find.' While the idea of receiving divine help reaches its height and glory in the Gospels, it did not, of course, arise there; long before that the psalmist was singing:

I will lift up mine eyes unto the hills, from whence cometh my help. My help cometh from the Lord (Psalm 121).

'The thing is immemorial and universal' as Aldous Huxley says in the introduction to his *The Perennial Philosophy* (1947); 'Rudiments of . . . [it] may be found among the traditionary lore of primitive peoples in every region of the world, and in its fully developed form it has a place in every one of the higher religions.'

I am often asked 'Can anything be said about a possible purpose in the universe?' I gave some kind of a reply to this question in the last chapter of my book *The Divine Flame*; I will use almost the same words in replying to it now. I think most agnostics and humanists, if asked, would say 'No'. Now I admit that I don't think anything *useful* can be said, because it can be nothing more than the wildest possible speculation; nevertheless perhaps it might just be worth saying that, on purely logical grounds, it is not impossible to imagine a reasonable goal for the cosmic evolutionary process. Certainly any such guess made in the twentieth century is most unlikely to be the correct one; however – and I think perhaps *this* is worth saying – the very fact that one can conceive an even remotely possible solution may save one from being in the pessimistic position of imagining that there can be *no possible purpose* in the process at all. Such a defeatist loss of all sense of meaning in the world is one of the tragic outcomes of the materialism of today.

My tentative and no doubt entirely improbable answer cannot be other than a quite fantastic flight of fancy into the realm of science fiction. Perhaps I am making a great mistake and am simply making myself ridiculous. I take the risk of this because without outlining the idea, which I agree is no doubt almost absurd, one cannot vindicate one's believe that *logically* it is not impossible to conceive of a cosmic plan in the evolutionary process. So with this warning of what nonsense to expect, I will apologetically proceed.

We see the continually increasing rate of man's scientific and technological skill and achievements. The progress in the present century is staggering. All this great development has come about in an extraordinary short space of time and indeed the whole of man's civilization is but a few thousand years compared with the two thousand million years' span of organic evolution. Provided we have no cosmic or man-made disaster, we should, on this earth alone, still have more than a thousand million years of evolution in front of us. Consider this acceleration of our material progress. Seventy-five years ago man had only just learnt to fly; he had just flown the English Channel. Today millions of people fly every year across the oceans of the world and the pioneers are now out in space and have landed on the moon. Who can doubt that within a few hundred years man will be in every part of the solar system in which he can get a footing by building elaborate, air-filled, cooled or heated capsules. There is the same progress in almost every field. Animal life can now be suspended by freezing only to start again into full vigour by appropriate thawing techniques. Man, by being drugged and put under improved techniques of suspended animation will no doubt be sent unconscious in capsules to be brought to life again in perhaps thousands of years' time when he has reached far away parts of the galaxy. With potentially some *thousand million* years of time in front of him, the mind boggles at the thought of what or where he might be. There is no need to enlarge on it, except in one direction, and that is in the development of computers – great exosomatic brains; see how they have increased in size and operational possibilities in just *ten* years' time. What will they be like in a *million* years' time?

So much for the physical side for which, I believe, no such picture need be an exaggeration; it is on the other side where speculation must be folly. I am optimistic enough to expect that man's spiritual and intellectual life (if we can still call him man!) – with a greatly extended natural theology – will also have developed enormously. Given sufficient time and a sufficient increase in information – stored mechanically for reference far beyond the memories of individual men – it seems possible that there must logically come a point when man has indeed asked every possible question that can be asked and has in time gained and recorded every possible answer. He will know all the secrets of the universe. He may in addition have developed a new collective consciousness and a greatly increased spirituality. I am, perhaps, in my imaginary answer getting near the Omega point of Teilhard de Chardin, but by a different road. Perhaps indeed we really *are* the children of God and that evolution must, with its spiritual element operating within the material matrix, eventually lead to a collective omniscient consciousness knowing just how and where in the universe life may and *will* be started again! We are perhaps part of a great system for generating love, joy and beauty in the universe: the highlights of existence that can only be perceived and appreciated when seen against the darker background of their opposites. You may remember that I heretically think it likely that love, joy and beauty are not only generated but *felt* (who knows?) far down in the animal world, and that man alone has come to discuss and express them in words. Yes, to imagine a purpose is not impossible; but to suppose that what we imagine *is* actually the real purpose would be the height of impertinence. Let us leave it at that and return to earth; we may return full of a confidence that, from what the mystics, poets and artists tell us, the real meaning of the cosmic process is something far more wonderful than anything we can possibly imagine in our present state of being.

Let me end the book with part of the quotation from the autobiography of Alfred Russel Wallace which I gave on p. 76. He was comparing his views on evolution with those of Darwin and says regarding man 'that while his body was undoubtedly developed by the continuous modification of some ancestral animal form, some different agency, analagous to that which first produced organic *life* and then originated *consciousness* came into play in order to develop the higher intellectual and spiritual nature of man'.

That is Darwinism with a difference.

INDEX